Your Will and What To Do About It

Your Will And What To Do About It

Samuel G. Kling

FOLLETT PUBLISHING COMPANY   Chicago

Second printing

© Copyright 1971 by Samuel G. Kling. All rights reserved. No portion of this book may be reproduced in any form without written permission of the publisher. Manufactured in the United States of America.

Library of Congress Catalog Card Number: 77-113714
ISBN 0-695-80212-7

To my parents, who left a legacy of love

Note To The Reader

Your Will and What To Do About It is the latest in a series of books the author has written interpreting and simplifying law for the layman and is in some ways the most important. Your will is a momentous document. By means of it you leave instructions for disposing of your property after you're gone.

The aim of this book is to provide simple, lucid answers to the many questions people ask about wills, and it has general applicability throughout the United States.

To this end the text defines many of the key terms used in wills and their administration, discusses at some length the importance of wills, describes who gets what if you leave no will, answers the question of whether or not you should write your own will and under what circumstances, lists some of the important duties of executors, and offers some practical suggestions on what to leave and how to leave it.

In addition, the book describes the role of trusts and trustees, illustrates how to revoke or change your will, discusses the meaning of probate, explains how an estate is distributed or settled, how long it takes, and what it costs.

If *Your Will and What To Do About It* sheds some light for the layman on the dark areas of wills and probate, the aim of the author will be realized.

Samuel G. Kling

Contents

CHAPTER 1

DEFINING THE TERMS

The law of wills like other branches of knowledge has its own special vocabulary, a sort of legal shorthand which makes understandable that which is vague and esoteric. Certain key words and phrases will help you better understand wills and estates.

Abate—Reduce or cut down general legacies proportionately when assets are insufficient.

Ademption—A bequest which has failed or been revoked.

Ancestor—Any person from whom an inheritance is derived.

Ancestral estate—Estate owned by an ancestor.

Ancillary—Serving as an aid, auxiliary, secondary. A foreign secondary administrator is known as an Ancillary Administrator. If the testator has assets in a state other than the one in which he died and the state allows it, the original executor or administrator may obtain ancillary letters to collect those assets and may also request that an ancillary executor or administrator be appointed in the other state to collect those assets.

Administrator—One appointed by the probate court or its equivalent to settle an estate for someone who (1) died without a valid will, (2) though he had a will, failed to name an executor, (3) named an executor that failed or refused to qualify or failed to settle the estate. When there is a will but no executor, the court appoints an administrator c. t. a. (*cum testamento annexo* or "with the will annexed"). When an executor or an administrator c. t. a. begins the settlement of an estate under a will and dies or resigns or becomes disqualified, the court appoints an administrator c. t. a. d. b. n. (*cum testamento annexo de bonis non*), to complete the settlement of the estate. When there is no will and the administrator dies, resigns, or becomes disqualified, his successor is called an administrator d. b. n. (*de bonis non* or "of goods not administrated") of that part of the estate not settled.

Affinity—Relationship by marriage, such as brother-in-law or son-in-law.

Appurtenances—Everything that goes along with the land, privileges, rights, and improvements that belong to the principal property.

Bequeath—To give personal property by will.

Caveator—one seeking to upset a will.

Chose in action—(pronounced shōz) personal property that is intangible, that requires action to reduce it to possession. An example is a life insurance policy; it is not the paper itself that is valuable but the rights of the insured or beneficiary under the policy; even if the policy is destroyed, the beneficiary may recover. Other examples of choses in action are stocks and savings accounts, royalties due an author on a contract for his book, and damages from the negligent driver of the automobile that killed the deceased. In a will the testator may leave whatever rights he may have to recover a debt or receive money for breach of contract or receive damages for a tort connected with contract by using the convenient though technical phrase "and all other choses in action." Tort is a civil wrong such as slander or an act of negligence causing injury.

Codicil—Supplement or addition which adds to, modifies, changes, or takes something from the original will. It must be executed with all the formalities of a will. Without a will, there cannot be a codicil. If the will is invalid for any reason, so is the codicil.

Community property—Basically partnership property. Property acquired before the marriage belongs to each spouse separately. Property acquired by either spouse during marriage is community property. Even though one partner contributed nothing in the way of earnings during the marriage, that partner has a half interest in whatever property was acquired during wedlock. A spouse can dispose of his or her share of the community property by will. States which have community property are Arizona, California, Louisiana, Nevada, New Mexico, Texas, and Washington. Property acquired in a non-community property state such as New York does not become community property if the couple moves to California or Arizona.

Consanguinity—Relationship by blood, such as father and son.

Corporate executor—Trust company or bank named in the will to serve as executor.

Corporate trustee—Trust company, or bank with trust powers, serving as trustee.

Corpus—The principal of the estate.

Curtesy—The right a husband has in the real estate of his deceased wife. This varies among the states but is usually a life interest in the wife's real estate. A husband has no right of curtesy if the marriage is childless.

Descent—Real estate one receives from a person who dies without leaving a will.

Devise—To give real estate or lands by will.

Devisee—One to whom real estate is given.

Disbursement—Money paid out by an executor, administrator, trustee, or guardian by way of debts, assessments, charges, and other expenditures in the course of settlement or administration of an estate. A disbursement differs from a distribution. When an executor pays the funeral expenses, it is a disbursement; when he pays a legacy, it is a distribution.

Distribution—Passing of personal property of one who dies without a will to the next of kin. It is now commonly applied to the passing of personal property whether under will or under statutes of intestacy.

Distributee—One who takes personal property either by will or under the law. It is synonymous with legatee.

Domicile—Place where a person has his true, fixed, permanent home and principal establishment and to which, whenever he is absent, he has the intention of returning. One may have many residences, but only one domicile. You may have an apartment on Park Avenue, a summer home in Maine, and spend your winters in Montego Bay. If you consider your permanent home New York, vote and pay taxes there, then New York is your legal domicile, no matter how many other residences you maintain. Domicile is largely a matter of intent. Your intent however is inferred from such acts as voting and payment of taxes. Estates are distributed according to the laws of the state of one's domicile, not one's temporary residence.

Donee—One who receives a gift.

Donor—One who does the giving.

Dower—The right a widow has in the real estate of her deceased husband. It is usually a life estate in one-third of all the land her husband owns during the marriage. Dower cannot be willed because ownership ceases by the death of the widow. Dower no longer exists in Alaska, Arizona, California, Colorado, Connecticut, Indiana, Iowa, Kansas, Maine, Minnesota, Mississippi, Missouri, Nebraska, Nevada, New Mexico, North Carolina, North Dakota, Okahoma, Pennsylvania, South Dakota, Texas, Washington, and Wyoming. In place of dower a widow takes either under her husband's will or under the laws of the state in which her husband died.

Election—The right of a spouse to take his or her share under the will or, waiving such rights, under the laws of intestacy. The election must be made within a prescribed time ● and varies with the individual state.

Entail—Restricting an inheritance to a certain succession of heirs, such as limiting passage of title to male heirs.

Escheat—The reversion of property to the state when there are no heirs or devisees.

Executor—One named in the will to settle the estate. If more than one is named, they are co-executors. If a woman is named to settle the estate, she is an executrix.

Fee simple—Largest possible estate one can have in land, and implies absolute ownership. An estate left in fee simple is an inheritance clear of any condition, limitation, or restriction.

Guardian—One who has the legal care and management of the person or estate or both of a child during its minority, the child being the ward. The father, and on his death the mother, is the natural guardian of the person of the minor, but not of its property. The same individual, trust company, or bank may be the guardian of both the person and the property or one may be the guardian of the person and another the guardian of the property. Naming a trustee in the will eliminates the need for naming a guardian for the minor's portion of the estate. A trustee has wider discretion in the administration of a trust than does a guardian.

Heirs—Those taking real estate of one who dies without a will or who leaves a will and directs that it be divided according to law.

Heirloom—Personal chattel which goes along with the inheritance by special custom to the heir and not to the executor or administrator.

Holographic will—One written entirely by the hand of the testator. It may be written in pencil, in ink, or partly in both. It may take the form of a letter or a note. It must be entirely written, signed, and dated by the testator. Holographic wills are valid in the following states.

Alaska No witnesses required.

Arizona No witnesses.

Arkansas Three disinterested witnesses.

California No witnesses.

Idaho No witnesses.

Kentucky No witnesses.

Louisiana No witnesses.

Mississippi No witnesses.

Montana No witnesses.

Nevada No witnesses.

New York Holographic wills by soldiers while in actual military service or by sailors while at sea are valid during the war, whether declared or not. Such wills become unenforceable and invalid one year after the testator's discharge from military service provided the testator still retains the capacity to make a will. If a testator lacks such capacity, the holographic will is valid and enforce-

able until one year after the capacity is regained.
North Carolina It must appear that the will was
found among the testator's papers. Testator's hand-
writing must be proved by three witnesses.
North Dakota No witnesses.
Oklahoma No witnesses.
Pennsylvania No witnesses.
Puerto Rico No witnesses.
South Dakota No witnesses.
Tennessee Substantially the same provisions as
are in force in North Carolina.
Texas No witnesses.
Utah No witnesses.
Virginia No witnesses.
West Virginia No witnesses.
Wyoming No witnesses.

Intestate—One who dies without leaving a valid will.
Dying without a will is called intestacy.

Issue—Legitimate child or children of a marriage. The
word includes grandchildren.

Kindred—A group of blood related persons.

Last will and testament—At one time a will disposed
of real estate and a testament disposed of personal
property. Today both dispose of any and all kinds of
property to take effect upon death, so "Will" and
"Last will and testament" mean exactly the same
thing.

Legacy—Gift of personal property by will. One who
receives such a gift is called a legatee.

Letters of administration—Certificate of the probate
court that the administrator named has qualified and
is authorized to proceed with the settlement of the
estate. Certificates, whether of letters testamentary or
of administration, are the passports of executors and
administrators. Without them neither is able to func-

tion. With them they can draw out deposits, have stock transferred, and carry out any action in connection with the estate.

Letters testamentary—Certificate of the probate court that the executor named in the will has qualified and is authorized to proceed with the settlement of the estate according to the terms of the will. See Letters of administration.

Life estate—Real estate which passes for life only, as a life estate in a house to one's daughter and upon her death to her son. The daughter is the life tenant, the son the remainderman.

Lineal descent—Direct line of descent, such as a child or grandchild.

Next of kin—Those taking the personal property of one who dies without a will or who makes a will and directs that it be divided according to law. To determine your heirs you must first learn from the laws of your state who would take your real property without a will. To determine your next of kin you must similarly learn who would get your personal property if you died without a will.

Nuncupative will—An oral one made during the last illness of the deceased in the presence of witnesses disposing of his personal property after death. Soldiers in actual military service and sailors at sea may verbally dispose of their wages and personal property in any amount if they are in actual fear or peril of death or in expectation of immediate death from an injury received that day. Such a will should be employed as a last resort. It is valid in the following states.

Alabama Valid only when the personal property bequeathed does not exceed $500. Such a will must be made during the last illness of the deceased at his dwelling or where he resided ten days or more, except when the testator is taken ill away from home and dies before his return. It must be shown that the deceased called upon persons present, or some of them, to bear witness that the statement is his will. Oral wills made by soldiers in actual military service or sailors at sea are also valid in Alabama.

Alaska Permitted if the deceased's words or the substance thereof are reduced to writing within thirty days after they are spoken and the writing probated after fourteen days and within six months after such words are spoken. Any sailor at sea or soldier in military service may dispose verbally of his wages or other personal property.

Arizona Allowed if made in the last illness of the deceased when the property does not exceed $50. The amount disposed of is unlimited if three competent witnesses testify that the testator called on some person to take notice and bear witness that such is his will and that the testimony or its substance was reduced to writing within six days.

Arkansas Must be made at time of last illness of deceased in the presence of at least two witnesses. The amount is limited to $500. Such a will must be reduced to writing and signed by the witnesses within fifteen days and must be proved between twenty days and six monthss after it is made.

California The amount is limited to $1,000. The will must be proved by two witnesses present, one of whom was asked by the testator at the time to bear witness that such was his will. In addition, the deceased must have been in actual military service in the field or at sea and in actual fear or peril of death or in expectation of immediate death from an injury received that day. The verbal statement of the deceased must be reduced to writing within thirty days after the making.

Delaware Valid if confined to personal property not exceeding $200. It must have been pronounced in the last illness of the deceased before two witnesses, be reduced to writing within three days, and be attested by the signatures of the witnesses if the testator dies before the expiration of the said three days or subsequently becomes incapable of making a will.

District of Columbia Invalid except in the case of soldiers and sailors in actual military service who may dispose of wages and personal property by word of mouth. Such a will must be proved by two witnesses and reduced to writing within ten days after its making.

Florida Must be proved by three witnesses present at the time of making. The oral will must have been made during the deceased's last illness and be reduced to writing within six days of its making. Personal property only may be disposed of in this way.

Georgia Must be made during the last illness of the deceased at the place where he resided for at least ten days preceding the declaration, except in case of sudden illness and death away from home. Three witnesses are necessary to prove such a will.

Idaho Must be reduced to writing within thirty days of its making. The will must be probated not less than fourteen days after the testator's death.

Indiana Must be made in the testator's last illness, be witnessed by at least two people, and be reduced to writing within fifteen days after the words are spoken. Such a will is valid up to $100 worth of personal property.

Iowa Personal property up to $300 may be disposed of by an oral will if witnessed by two competent persons. Those in actual military or naval service may dispose of all their personal estate orally.

Kansas To be valid an oral will must be reduced to writing and witnessed by two disinterested persons within ten days after the words are spoken. It must be proved that the testator called upon some person or persons present to bear witness that the words were his last will.

Kentucky Only a soldier in actual service or a sailor at sea may dispose of personal effects orally, provided it is done ten days before his death, in the presence of two competent witnesses, and reduced to writing within sixty days after the words are spoken.

Louisiana Must be witnessed in the presence of a notary public by three persons residing in the place where the will is executed, or by five persons not residing in the place.

Maine Allowed when made in the last illness of the testator at his home or at the place where he resided ten days before making it and the maximum amount is $100. The will must be proved by three witnesses who were requested at the time of making by the testator to bear witness that such was his will. If the words are not reduced to writing within six days after being spoken, they must be proved in court within six months. A soldier in actual service or a sailor at sea may orally dispose of his personal estate.

Maryland Valid only for soldiers in actual service or sailors at sea, who may dispose of their wages, movables, and personal property.

Massachusetts Same as for Maryland.

Michigan   Anyone may will orally a maximum of $300. The will must be proved by two competent witnesses.

Mississippi   Valid only when made during the testator's last illness. Maximum amount is $100 unless the will is proved by two witnesses whom the testator called to bear witness to his will. Such a will cannot be proved after six months unless reduced to writing within six days of speaking.

Missouri   The maximum amount to be disposed of may not exceed $200; two witnesses must prove that the testator in his last sickness, at his home, called some person to witness the will. Proof of such will must be given within six months after the words are spoken or the substance of the words reduced to writing within thirty days. Wills of soldiers and sailors are governed by the common law.

Montana   Valid when proved by two witnesses present at the making. One at least must have been asked by the testator to bear witness that such was his will, and the maximum value is $1,000. The testator at the time must have been in actual military or marine service, and the will must have been made in the expectation of immediate death from injury received that day. The will must be proved within six months after it was made, but not less than fourteen days after the death of the testator.

Nebraska   The maximum amount that can be willed orally is $150. The will must be proved by three witnesses who were called by the testator to witness his oral will during his last illness at home or while taken sick away from home. Unless reduced to writing within six days after the oral declaration, the will is not allowed. These rules are applicable to soldiers and sailors in actual service.

Nevada The maximum value that can be willed orally is $1,000. The will must be made during the testator's last illness and proved by two witnesses present at the making not less than fourteen days nor more than three months after the words are spoken.

New Hampshire The maximum value that can be willed orally is $100. The will must be declared in the presence of three witnesses and made during testator's last illness, at his usual dwelling place unless he is taken ill while away from home and dies before his return. A memorandum of the oral will must be reduced to writing within six days after death and presented to the probate court within six months after the making.

New Jersey Bequeathing personal property exceeding $80 is invalid unless proved by the oaths of at least three witnesses present at the making thereof and unless the testator requested the persons present to bear witness to his verbal will or words to that effect. The will must be made during the testator's last illness, in his house or where he was a resident for ten days or more except when the deceased was taken sick while away from his home and died before returning.

New York Only soldiers in service and sailors at sea may bequeath personal property by oral will. It must be made within the hearing of two persons and its execution proved by at least two witnesses.

North Carolina An oral will must be proved by at least two witnesses present at the time it was made. The will must have been made during the testator's last sickness and where he had been residing.

North Dakota The maximum amount that can be willed orally is $1,000. The will must be proved by two witnesses who were present at its making; the deceased must have been in actual military service in the field or doing duty on shipboard at sea and in fear or peril of immediate death from an injury received the same day that the will was made.

Ohio Must be made in the last illness of the testator; it must be reduced to writing and subscribed to by two competent witnesses within ten days after the verbal declaration.

Oklahoma The maximum amount that can be willed orally is $1,000. The will must be proved by two witnesses who were present at the making thereof, one of whom was asked by the testator at the time to act as a witness. In addition, the testator must have been in actual military service in the field or doing duty on shipboard at sea and in actual fear or peril of death from an injury received that same day.

Oregon Valid only for soldiers in service and sailors at sea.

Pennsylvania Valid if made by those in imminent peril of death, whether from illness or otherwise, and only if testator died of the peril. The will must be declared to be such before two disinterested witnesses, reduced to writing within ten days after such declaration, and submitted to probate within three months of death. Such wills are void if they dispose of more than $500 of either personal property or real estate. Such a will does not revoke or change an existing written will.

South Carolina Disposing of personal property in excess of $50 is invalid unless proved by the oaths of three or more witnesses who were present when the will was made and requested by the testator to witness his will. The will must be made in the testator's last illness and in his house or place where he died. Proof of such will cannot be made after six months from the time the words were spoken unless reduced to writing within six days after the making of such will and then not after one year.

South Dakota The maximum amount that can be willed orally is $1,000. The will must be proved by two witnesses present at the time the words were spoken.

Texas Valid if made during the last illness of the deceased, at his home unless he was taken sick away from home and died before returning. No oral will is allowed when the personal property bequeathed exceeds $30 in value unless proved by three credible witnesses. The will must be proved within fourteen days of the testator's death and not after six months from the date of speaking, unless committed to writing within six days therefrom.

Utah If the estate is not in excess of $1,000, an oral will may be admitted to probate at any time after the words are spoken; the words must be reduced to writing within thirty days after they are spoken.

Vermont May not pass personal possessions exceeding $200 in value. A memorandum in writing must be made by a person present at the time of making within six days.

Virginia Only soldiers in military service and sailors at sea may dispose of personal property by oral will.

Washington Allowed if the personal estate does not exceed $200. The will must be made during the testator's last illness and must be proved by two witnesses who were requested by the testator to witness his will. The will must be reduced to writing.

West Virginia   Only soldiers and sailors in actual service may dispose of personal property by an oral will.

Wisconsin   Disposing of an estate in excess of $150 is of no effect unless proved by the oath of three witnesses, present when the will was made, who were requested by the testator to witness it. It must be made during the last illness of the testator, in his dwelling or where he resided for ten days prior to the making of the will unless he was taken sick while absent from his home and died before returning.

Per capita—Receiving as an individual and not as a representative of an ancestor. A testator survived by three children and three grandchildren declared in his will that his own children and the children of his deceased son share equally in the estate. The estate would then be divided into six parts and each child and grandchild would receive an equal share, that is, one sixth of the total estate. See per stirpes.

Per stirpes—Receiving by right of representation or by virtue of standing in the shoes of some ancestor. For example, in his will a testator directs that his estate be divided equally among his children. He is survived by three living children and one dead son who has three children. The estate is then divided into four parts, each of the three living children receiving one-fourth of the total estate and the remaining one-fourth being divided equally for each of the three grandchildren, who will receive one-twelfth of the total estate. The grandchildren by virtue of representing their dead father receive only what he would have received had he been alive at the time of the distribution. See per capita.

Personal property—A wide ranging term that includes anything not real estate. Examples are automobiles, stereo sets, TV sets, furniture, clothing, tools, stocks, books, and bonds.

Posthumous child—One born after the father's death.

Probate—Legal establishment of the validity of a will.

Real estate—This includes not only the land itself but the house which stands on it as well as fences, growing trees, and other things attached to the land.

Residuary legatee—One who receives the balance of an estate after payment of claims, expenses, taxes, and all other specified legacies.

Residue or residuary estate—That which is left after all debts and expenses have been paid and all bequests and devises distributed. The usual description of the residuary estate is as follows: "All the rest, residue, and remainder of my property, real, personal, and mixed, of every kind, nature, and description and wherever situated, of which I shall die seized and possessed, or to which I shall be in any way entitled, including any estate to which I shall have the power of disposition or appointment at the time of my death, I give devise and bequeath to———." The purpose of inserting a residuary paragraph is to make certain that all of the testator's property is legally disposed of, so that nothing passes under the laws of intestacy.

Spouse—Either husband or wife.

Testamentary disposition—The disposition of property either by will or codicil. It is usually found in wills in connection with the revocation of former wills and codicils. For example, "I hereby revoke all former wills and codicils and other testamentary dispositions made by me." A testamentary disposition may also include a living trust made in contemplation of or to take effect only after the testator's death.

Testator—A man who makes a will.

Testatrix—A woman who makes a will.

Trustee—One who takes legal title to property to hold or administer for the benefit of another. A trustee under a will may be named by the testator or appointed by the court. Occasionally a testator creates a trust without naming a trustee or names a trustee who dies or refuses to accept the trust or, having accepted it, is later removed. The probate court, rather than let the trust fail for lack of a trustee, will name a trustee to carry out the terms of the trust set forth in the will.

The same person, trust company, or bank may be both executor or administrator c. t. a. and trustee. If the same trust company or bank is both executor and trustee, it must first settle the estate as executor and make the distribution to itself as trustee, as it would to any other beneficiary. After it gets its discharge as executor, it then enters its duties as trustee as if two different persons or corporations were acting, one as executor, the other as trustee.

CHAPTER 2

THE IMPORTANCE OF WILLS

Man is born, lives, loves, works, and dies. If he is lucky and enterprising, he accumulates what the law calls an "estate."

A good dictionary gives the word a variety of meanings.

It may be a period or condition of life, as when one attains to "man's estate." It may refer to a specific political, social, or professional group such as the fourth estate of journalism. More commonly, however, estate refers to a piece of landed property, especially one with an expensive house, such as a country estate. It also refers to the degree or quantity of interest you may have in land, such as a life estate or an estate for a limited number of years.

But in this book and for our purposes we mean by estate the property or possessions a person has at the time of his death. The estate may be large or small. It may run into millions, like those left by Rockefellers, Fords, and Kennedys. Or it may have a net worth of a few hundred dollars. It may consist of vast holdings of real property or the small house in which you and your wife live. It may contain stocks and bonds, insurance policies, a checking or savings account, paintings, jewelry, furs, and books or merely a few heirlooms that have been handed down to you from generation to generation.

In short, whatever you leave at the time of your death—whether large or small—constitutes your estate. And this is what we are going to talk about.

Now it is one thing to accumulate property and possessions and quite another thing to know what to do about them. Consider some of the alternatives:

1. You can follow the advice of Jesus and give everything to the poor.

2. You can place everything you own in joint names.

3. You can die intestate, that is without bothering to write a will, in which case your property will be distributed according to the laws of intestacy of your particular state. This may or may not fit your individual needs.

4. You can have a competent lawyer prepare a will for you.

If you follow the first course, you may be regarded as an eccentric, and you will be reduced to penury. If money means nothing to you and you consider your family an encumbrance or nuisance, this may be a solution. All you have to do is divest yourself of the trappings of civilization including its comforts and pleasures and live the rest of your life under a palm tree in some remote desert isle. Things being what they are in this year of our Lord, such a plan admittedly has some attractions!

If you are married and have a trusting nature, you can place everything you have jointly in your name and that of your spouse as tenants by the entireties with right of survivorship. Such a tenancy has certain advantages. For one thing you won't need a will and can avoid the expense of an attorney as well as the costs of probate and administration. Should you die while such a tenancy is in effect, your house, stocks, bonds, and money jointly owned in savings and checking accounts automatically goes to your spouse.

On the other hand, your children will receive nothing under such an arrangement, nor will your ailing mother, your favorite brother or sister, or your pet charity. Your spouse gets it all, and your youngsters and parents are dependent on your widow for their future support and well being.

Suppose, for example, that after a decent period of mourning a widow remarries and has children by the new husband. In that case the second husband gets a portion of the property as do the offspring of that marriage, so that total strangers acquire a share of your estate.

But even while you live there may be serious objections to holding everything in joint names. Probably the most important is that under such a plan you lose some control of your property. You may wish to sell a particular security at a certain time but must first obtain your spouse's signature. Should you disagree with each other about the advisability of such a sale at this particular time, either out of business logic or emotional suspicion, the security cannot be sold.

How much of your assets should be held jointly depends on a number of facts. What may be appropriate for a couple who have overcome the storms and stresses of marriage may be highly inappropriate for a couple always on the verge of divorce. What may be right for a prudent, thoughtful, affectionate spouse may be singularly wrong for a giddy, loveless, and promiscuous one. Each marriage and each case must be judged on its own merits. It is one thing when the wife has made a genuine contribution either by way of earnings or by devotion to the family; it is different when there is mistrust, distaste, and hostility. Many marriages are fragile, and roughly one in three end in annulment, desertion, separation, or divorce. This could mean that if a wife owned a half interest in all her husband's assets including his business, he might find himself in an impossible financial situation should the marriage break down.

Just as the prudent investor refrains from placing all his investment eggs in one basket, so the prudent man or woman might refrain from putting all their assets in joint names. This does not necessarily mean that nothing should be jointly owned. There is no reason, for example, why the family house and a modest checking and savings account should not be held as tenants by the entireties. But if some assets are in joint names and some in one name, you will need a will.

What happens if you die intestate, that is without a will? First, the law appoints the administrator of your estate, usually the surviving husband or wife. Either one, no matter how amiable and loving, may lack the necessary skill, experience, and competence or may not have the requisite judgment.

Second, your spouse's share may be smaller than you intended. Many people have the curious notion that upon the death of one spouse, where there is no will everything automatically goes to the other. This just is not true. In cases of intestacy the surviving spouse gets only one-third to one-half of whatever is left, depending on the laws of the particular state. The rest may go to children, parents, sisters, brothers, nieces, and nephews.

Third, when there is no will, all children get equal treatment. One child may be well, another ill; one devoted, another hostile; one child thrifty, another extravagant. One youngster may be married to a devoted husband and father, another wed to a philandering wastrel. Where there is no will, in the eyes of the law each child is entitled to receive exactly the same share of the parent's estate, regardless of individual needs or differences.

Fourth, where there is no will, the inheritance of your youngsters is affected. If they are minors they will be able to inherit property but not use it until they are twenty-one. The appointment of a guardian, of having him file a bond, make periodic accountings for acts performed on behalf of the minors, and obtain the court's approval for services proposed on their behalf all takes time and money.

Fifth, administrating the estate could well be more expensive. To protect the beneficiaries as well as the creditors most states insist that the administrator be bonded, costs of which must come out of the estate.

Sixth, the administrator is not a free agent. He is limited by law with sometimes unhappy consequences. For instance, an administrator is restricted as to the type of investment he can make on behalf of an estate. He may be forced to sell high grade securities in a bear market, or wind up a going, profitable business to the loss of all concerned.

Seventh, there may be unnecessary taxes because without a will matters are left to chance. Your spouse may receive less than the full amount that could have been given tax free. Your parents, already wealthy, may pay additional taxes because through intestacy they receive a substantial portion of your estate.

Consider, now, the advantages of having your attorney prepare your will. First, a will is a plan or design for the distribution of property you have acquired through blood, sweat, and tears. It is made especially for you, like a custom tailored suit, and can represent the best thought of both you and your counsel as to how your money might be distributed after your death.

By means of a will you can choose your beneficiaries, whether spouse, parents, brothers, sisters, friends, employees, or favorite charity. You can determine in advance, knowing that your wishes will be carried out, what portion of your property you wish each person to have, if any. In other words, you can take individual needs and circumstances into consideration. You can provide generously for the spouse who has contributed much to your happiness and to that of your family, or you can provide only the minimum the law allows for one who has made your life a living hell. You can take care of an indigent parent who requires attention in his declining years or of a child who is mentally and physically disabled.

Equally important, a will allows you to choose how and when your beneficiaries are to receive their share of your estate. It may be folly to leave an entire estate outright to someone who has no flair for business; it may be reckless to leave a large sum of money outright to someone whose only talent is to spend it foolishly and fast. Leaving in trust the bulk of a large estate provides an income rather than only principal to be consumed quickly. Preparing your will with the aid of a skilled attorney gives you the opportunity of bequeathing your own best judgment as to the needs and capacity of those closest and dearest to you.

A second reason for having a will is the saving on administration expenses. For example, you can waive the requirement that the executor or trustee post a bond. In a substantial estate such a bond may run into thousands of dollars. Even in a small estate the cost may run into several hundred dollars. You can grant your executor or trustee the power to sell real estate and save the costs of each judicial authorization and approval.

Third, you can choose as your executor the person

or persons you think most qualified to handle your affairs after your death. An executor has greater flexibility than a court-appointed administrator and can do more things more easily, without running into court frequently for judicial authorization or approval. He can, for instance, maintain and develop your property and sell only as market conditions warrant. He may elect not to sell your securities if they are in a depressed state. He need not wind up a going, profitable business if its continuance is in the best interests of the beneficiaries. You decide whether the executor is clothed with broad and elastic powers or with narrow, confining ones.

An efficient and experienced executor can actually enhance the value of your estate by resisting unjust claims, reducing taxes to the legal minimum, and enforcing whatever claims the estate has against third parties either by settlement or suit. He can conserve the estate's assets by economizing on expenses, and he can give attention to the needs of the beneficiaries.

To recapitulate, a will offers a number of advantages:

1. A will allows you to arrange for the distribution of all your assets to fit the exact needs of your family.

2. A will allows you to make different provisions for sons and daughters no matter how divergent their individual circumstances.

3. A will gives you freedom to leave assets in trust under experienced financial and investment management for those members of your family who would most benefit.

4. Without a will the state distributes your assets; with a will you can select, appoint, and instruct an executor as to how you wish your assets to be managed.

5. With a will you can provide funds for the education of children and grandchildren; for the use of principal in case of illness, inflation, or other need or emer-

gency; and for the distribution of particular objects such as heirlooms, paintings, or a stamp or book collection.

6. A will can prevent your estate from going to strangers who might get it under the laws of intestacy.

Chapter 3

WHO GETS WHAT IF YOU LEAVE NO WILL

As pointed out briefly in the last chapter if there is no will, your property will be distributed according to the laws of intestacy prevailing in your particular state. Here for easy reference are the laws of descent and distribution for the fifty jurisdictions. Read the provisions of your own state and then make up your mind whether you want your property distributed according to the laws of your domicile or according to your own individual needs. Your decision may have far reaching consequences.

Alabama The real estate of a married man with children is divided equally among the children subject to a wife's dower, that is, her life interest in one-third or one-half the real estate. Other property, where there are less than five children, goes to the wife and children equally. If there are five or more children, one-fifth goes to the wife, the rest to the children equally. All the real estate of a married woman with children goes to the husband for life and then is equally divided among the children. Personal property goes one-half to the husband and one-half divided equally among the children.

The real estate of a married man without children goes to his parents equally, subject to the wife's dower.

All other property goes to the wife. A wife's real estate goes to her parents equally, subject to her husband's life interest. Personal property goes one-half to the husband, one-fourth to the father, and one-fourth to the mother.

Where the owner is either a widow or widower with children, the property goes to the children equally. If the deceased is single or a widow or widower without children, one-half of the property goes to each parent. If only one parent is living, he receives one-half and the other half is divided equally among brothers, sisters, and their descendants.

Alaska   If there are no children, the surviving spouse gets the entire estate. If the deceased leaves children, the surviving spouse takes one-half the real estate and one-half the personal property. Subject to the rights of the surviving spouse, the property is distributed as follows: One-half to surviving spouse and remainder, or all if no surviving spouse, to children and child of deceased child. If no children survive, property goes to grandchildren equally; to parents equally or survivor of them; to brothers and sisters or descendants of brothers and sisters; finally, to next of kin or to those claiming through nearest ancestor.

Arizona   Half the community property goes automatically to surviving spouse, the other half is subject to the will of the deceased. If there is no will, the property goes to the direct descendants of the deceased equally or to the survivor of them. Of the separate estate, where there is a surviving spouse and children, two-thirds of the real and personal property go to the children and one-third to the surviving spouse. Where there are no children but a surviving spouse, the personal property goes to the husband or wife, while one-half of the real property goes to the parents or survivor of them and the other half to the surviving spouse.

Arkansas A husband or wife has a life interest in a third of all real estate owned by the deceased spouse and a third interest in personal property, the children getting the rest. Where intestate left no descendants or kindred and has been continuously married not less than three years before death, surviving spouse takes all. If continuously married less than three years before death, spouse takes half, the rest going to other surviving kin in the following order: parents, brothers and sisters, grandfathers, uncles, aunts, and descendants of any such deceased.

California The rules of community property apply, half of the estate automatically going to the surviving spouse. Where there is no will and only a spouse, he or she receives all community property as well as separate property. Where there is a spouse and one child, the spouse receives all the community property and half the separate property. Where there is more than one child, the spouse receives all the community property and one-third of the separate property.

Colorado The entire estate of an intestate goes to the surviving husband or wife if there are no children. If there are children, one-half goes to the surviving spouse and the other half to the child, children, or grandchildren.

Connecticut When there are a surviving spouse and children, the spouse gets one-third of both real and personal property, the children two-thirds distributed equally. When there is no surviving spouse, the entire estate is divided equally among the children and representatives of deceased children, per stirpes. Where there is a surviving husband or wife but no children, and either one or both parents, the surviving spouse gets $5000 and one-half of the residue; where there are two surviving parents each receives one-half of the balance, i.e., one quarter of the estate; where there is only one surviving parent, he or she gets half the residue. Where there is no child, descendant, or parent, the surviving spouse gets the entire estate.

Delaware   One-half of the real estate goes to the surviving spouse for life, the balance goes to the child or children, the descendants of a deceased child taking a child's share among themselves. One-third of the personal property goes to the surviving spouse, two-thirds to child or children and descendants of deceased child or children. A widow or widower's real estate and personal property goes to the children and descendants of a deceased child or children. The real property of a single person or a widow or widower without children or grandchildren, goes to the parents; if one of them is dead, it goes to the survivor. One-half of the personal property goes to the mother, one-half to the father. If one of them is dead, all goes to the survivor. If both parents are dead, the personal property goes to brothers and sisters equally, the descendants of a deceased brother or sister taking his share by representation.

District of Columbia   Surviving spouse is entitled to one-third interest in real estate for life (dower) and half of the personal property. Where there are a surviving spouse and children, the former receives dower rights plus one-third of the personal property, the children getting the remainder.

Florida   All property goes to the surviving spouse and child or children in equal shares. Grandchildren take their deceased parent's share. The entire estate of a person without descendants goes to the surviving spouse. If the deceased is unmarried or a widow or widower without descendants, the father gets one-half, the mother the other half. If only one parent survives, he or she takes the entire estate. If there is no surviving spouse and no parents, the estate is divided among brothers and sisters in equal shares, the nieces and nephews taking their deceased parent's share.

Georgia　One-third of the real estate of a married man with children goes to the wife; two-thirds is equally divided among the children. Personal property is equally divided among wife and children. The property of a married woman with children is equally divided among husband and children. The property of a widow or widower with no children or grandchildren is equally divided among father, mother, brothers, and sisters; this also applies to an unmarried person. The property of a widow or widower with neither children nor grandchildren and without parents is equally divided among brothers and sisters. If there are no children, the entire estate goes to the surviving spouse.

Hawaii　The ownership of real estate is divided among the children. Two-thirds of the deceased's income is divided among the children and one-third goes to the spouse for life. Two-thirds of other assets are divided among the children while one-third goes outright to the surviving spouse. If there are no children, one-half of the estate goes to parents or survivor, the other half to the surviving spouse. In the case of a widow, widower, or divorcee with children the estate is divided equally among the children. In the case of an unmarried person, widow, widower, or divorcee with neither child nor grandchild, the entire estate goes to the parents or the survivor of them.

Idaho　In this community property state half goes automatically to the surviving spouse. Where there is a spouse only, both the community and separate property go to either husband or wife. Where there are a spouse and one child, the spouse receives half the separate property and the child the remainder. Where there are a spouse and more than one child, the husband or wife receives one-third of the separate property, the children two-thirds.

Illinois   The spouse receives one-third of the estate, the child or children divide two-thirds. If there are no descendants, the surviving spouse gets the entire estate. If there are children but no husband or wife, the children receive the entire property. Where there are parents, brothers, sisters, nieces, and nephews but no surviving spouse, children, or grandchildren, the parents, brothers, sisters, nephews, and nieces take all. Parents, brothers, and sisters share equally except that if one parent is dead, the surviving parent takes a double portion. Descendants of a brother or sister take their parents share. Descendants of a dead child take their parent's portion.

Indiana   If there is a surviving spouse only, he receives the entire estate. If there are a surviving spouse and one child, one-half the net estate goes to the spouse, the other half to the child. If there is more than one child, the husband or wife gets one-third of the estate, the children two-thirds.

Iowa   Where there is a surviving spouse only, he gets $15,000 plus one-half of the remaining estate, the balance going to parents equally or to the surviving parent. Where there is a spouse and children, one-third of the estate and all exempt personal property goes to the husband or wife, the balance to the children equally.

Kansas   One-half of the estate goes to the surviving spouse, the other half to the child or children. If there is no surviving spouse, the entire estate goes to the children. If there is no surviving spouse or child, the estate goes to the parents or the survivor of them.

Kentucky One-half of the estate goes to the surviving spouse, the other half to the child or children equally. If the deceased is childless, one-half goes
to the husband or wife, the balance to parents equally
or to the survivor. If there are no surviving parents,
one-half goes to wife or husband, the other half to
brothers and sisters equally. If there are no parents,
brothers, sisters, nieces, or nephews, all goes to husband or wife. A widow or widower's estate is divided
equally among the children, if any, or to parents or surviving parent, or to brothers and sisters or their descendants.

Louisiana This is a community property state in
which half the community property automatically
goes to the surviving spouse. The other half also goes
to the surviving spouse if there are no descendants or
parents.

Maine The surviving spouse receives one-third of
the estate, the children two-thirds divided equally
among them. If there is no husband or wife, the child
or children receive all. Grandchildren take their dead
parent's share unless all children are dead, in which
case all grandchildren share equally if all are living. If
there are no children or descendants, the surviving
spouse receives seven-ninths of the real estate with the
mother and father receiving two-ninths divided equally
or two-ninths to survivor. If there are no surviving parents, the brothers and sisters receive the two-ninths of
the real estate divided equally. If there are no brothers
and sisters, the two-ninths goes to the grandparents or
survivor. Of property other than real estate the wife
or husband gets $10,000 plus one-half of the remainder
of the personal property, the mother and father receiving the other half divided equally or all to the survivor.
If there is neither wife, husband, children nor des-

cendant, the mother gets one-half and the father the other half of all property. If one parent and brothers and/or sisters survive, the mother or father receives one-half and the other half is divided equally among brothers and sisters.

Maryland   The wife or husband gets one-third while the child or children get two-thirds divided equally. Grandchildren take their deceased parent's share. A widow or widower's child, children, or descendants take all divided equally. If there are no children or descendants, the wife or husband gets half and the surviving parents or parent the other half. If there are only brothers and sisters, the wife or husband gets $4,000 plus one-half the residue, while the brothers and sisters receive the other half of the residue divided equally. Descendants of a deceased brother or sister take that share. If there are no surviving parents, brothers, sisters, or descendants of them, the entire estate goes to the husband or wife. If an unmarried person or a widow or widower without children or descendants has surviving parents, the property is equally divided between the parents or all to the survivor. If there are no parents, all goes to the brothers and sisters equally.

Massachusetts   If the deceased leaves kindred but no issue, surviving spouse receives $25,000 plus half of the real and personal property. If deceased leaves issue, surviving spouse gets one-third of estate, children the other two-thirds divided equally. If deceased leaves no children, grandchildren, brothers, or sisters, surviving spouse takes all.

Michigan   In the case of a married man or woman with no children, parents, brothers, sisters, nephews, or nieces the entire estate goes to the surviving spouse. If the deceased is a married man with no children, one-half of the real estate goes to the wife, the other half to the father, mother, or survivor; of the personal property $3,000 and one-half of the remainder go to the wife, the balance to father, mother, or survivor. If the deceased is a married woman with no children, half of the real estate and of the personal property go to father, mother, or survivor and the other half to the husband. If the deceased is a married man or woman with children, two-thirds of the estate is equally divided among the children wth one-third going to the surviving wife or husband. Where there are children but no surviving spouse, the entire estate is divided equally among the children. In the case of a single person or widow or widower without children, the entire estate goes to the parents or survivor. If neither father nor mother survive, the estate passes to brothers and sisters and children of deceased brothers and sisters.

Minnesota   Husband or wife gets half of the estate, a child the other half. If there is more than one child, surviving husband or wife takes one-third of the property, the children two-thirds equally.

Mississippi   The surviving spouse takes all if there are no children or grandchildren; where there is a child, the husband or wife takes a share equal to that of the child.

Missouri   If the deceased leaves a widow or widower without children, the surviving spouse receives one-half of the estate and the balance is divided equally among the surviving parents, brothers, and sisters. Where there are no children, parents, brothers, sisters, or their descendants, the widow or widower takes all. When the deceased leaves a widow or widower with children, one-half goes to the surviving spouse, the balance to the children and grandchildren. Where there is no surviving spouse, the children and grandchildren take all. Where there are no husband, wife, children, or descendants, the surviving parents, brothers, and sisters take all.

Montana   Where the deceased is survived by a spouse only, the widow or widower takes all the property. When the deceased leaves a spouse and one child, the widow or widower takes one-half and the child or his issue the balance. When there is a surviving spouse and more than one child, the widow or widower takes one-third of all property and the children or issue two-thirds. If there is neither spouse nor issue, all the property goes to the parent or parents. If the only survivors are brothers and sisters, all goes to them and their issue per stirpes.

Nebraska   Surviving spouse who is parent of all children of deceased takes as follows: one-third if there are two or more children or one child and issue of one or more deceased children; one-half if there is only one child or issue of only one deceased child. Surviving spouse takes one-fourth if survivor is not the parent of all the decedent's children and there is one or more children or issue of one or more deceased children. If decedent left no issue, surviving spouse takes one-half if decedent left blood relatives or entire estate if deceased left no such relatives. Where there are no children or descendants of children, property descends to parents or survivor, brothers and sisters and/or children of deceased brother or sister, or next of kin.

Nevada   In this community property state half the community property automatically goes to the surviving spouse. A surviving spouse without children gets both the separate and community property. If there is a spouse and one child, the surviving husband or wife gets all the community property and one-half of the separate property. If there is more than one child, the surviving spouse gets all the community property and one-third of the separate property.

New Hampshire A surviving spouse only, gets $10,000 plus $2,000 for each year of marriage plus one-half of the real and personal property. When there is a surviving spouse and children, the widow or widower gets one-third of the estate.

New Jersey When the survivor is a spouse with children and representatives of deceased children, all the real property goes to the children subject to any right of dower or curtesy. One-third of the personal property goes to husband or widow, two-thirds to the children. Where there are no children or descendants of children, the entire estate goes to the surviving spouse. Where the only survivors are children or grandchildren, the estate is divided equally among the children. Where the only survivors are parents and representatives of deceased children, all goes equally to parents, brothers and sisters, and representatives of deceased brothers or sisters.

New Mexico This is a community property state with all the community property going automatically to the surviving spouse. When there are no children, the widow or widower gets all the separate property. When there are children, the surviving husband or wife gets one-fourth of the separate estate and the remainder goes to the children.

New York The widow or widower gets $2,000 and one-half of the remaining estate, a child the other half. Where there is more than one child, the surviving husband or wife gets $2,000 and one-third of the remaining estate. When there is no surviving spouse, all goes to the surviving children. If there are no children or grandchildren but parents are living, the widow or widower receives $25,000 plus one-half of the residue of the estate and the other half goes to the parents or survivor. If there are no parents, children, or descendants, the entire estate goes to the widow or widower.

If the only survivors are brothers and sisters and their representatives, the entire estate goes to them.

North Carolina   When intestate is survived by spouse and children or descendants of deceased children, the widow or widower receives one-third of all property, the children and their descendants two-thirds. When the spouse is survived by one child or his descendants, the surviving husband or wife gets one-half and the balance goes to the issue. When no husband or wife survives, the children and their issue receive the entire estate.

North Dakota   Surviving spouse takes one-half if decedent leaves children, all up to $50,000 in value and one-half of excess if decedent leaves no issue but leaves father or mother, all up to $100,000 if no issue or parent, all up to $100,000 and one-half of excess if decedent leaves no issue or parent but does leave brother or sister or issue.

Ohio   Where the intestate is survived by spouse only, the surviving husband or wife takes all the property. When there is in addition a child or his issue, the widow or widower takes one-half of all property and the other half goes to the child or his issue per stirpes. Where there is more than one child, the husband or wife takes one-third of all the property and the children get two-thirds in equal shares per stirpes. Where there are a surviving spouse and parents but no children, the widow or widower takes three-fourths of all property, the parents or parent one-fourth. When there are children but no surviving spouse, all the property goes to the children in equal shares. When there are surviving parents but neither spouse nor children, the estate goes to the parents or parent. When only brothers and sisters survive, they take all in equal shares.

Oklahoma If there is a spouse only (no issue, no parents, no brother or sister) the surviving husband or wife takes all. If there is a spouse and one child or his issue, the husband or wife takes one-half of all property and the child or his issue take the remainder. If there is more than one child, the surviving spouse takes one-third of all property and the children or issue take two-thirds of all property in equal shares per stirpes. When there is a surviving spouse, parents, brothers and sisters, but no issue, the widow or widower takes one-half of all the property with the parents or survivor taking the other half. If both parents are dead, one-half goes to the decedent's brothers and sisters and their issue in equal shares per stirpes. When there are parents surviving but no spouse nor issue, all the property goes to the parents or parent. When only brothers and sisters survive, the property is divided equally among them per stirpes.

Oregon Surviving spouse takes only curtesy or dower if decedent left issue but takes all real estate if no issue are alive. As to personal property, surviving spouse gets one-half if decedent left issue or all if there are no children or grandchildren alive. The real estate goes first to children and their issue equally, next to surviving spouse, then to parents and finally to brothers and sisters.

Pennsylvania The surviving spouse receives one-third with two-thirds divided equally among the children or their descendants. If there is only one child, the spouse gets one-half and the child or its descendants get the other half. If there are no children or descendants, the spouse receives $20,000 plus one-half the balance of the estate and the parents or parent receive the other half. If no parent survives, the wife or husband receives $20,000 plus one-half the balance and the brothers and sisters share the remainder equally. Nieces and nephews take a deceased parent's share unless all brothers and sisters are dead, in which case all nieces and nephews share equally. If there is a child or children surviving but no husband or wife, the child or children receive all, divided equally. Where there's no surviving spouse and no children or descendants, parents or the survivor receive all. If no parent survives, brothers and sisters share equally.

Rhode Island   When an unmarried person dies without a will, real estate and personal property go to the parents in equal shares or to the surviving parent. If there are no parents, it goes to the brothers and sisters and their descendants. Where a widow or widower dies without a will, the estate goes to the children or their descendants in equal shares. If there are no children or descendants, then to the parents. Where a married person dies without a will leaving a widow or widower and blood relatives but no children, the spouse gets a life interest in all the real estate of the deceased. Upon petition filed within six months after death the probate court may allow or set off to the surviving spouse as absolute property any real estate of the decedent situated in Rhode Island to an amount not exceeding $25,000 over and above all encumbrances, if such real estate is not required for payment of debts of the decedent. Subject to the above, the real estate goes to the parents in equal shares or to the surviving parent. If there are no parents, then to brothers and sisters and their descendants.

As to personal property, upon petition filed within six months after the appointment of an administrator the probate court may make an award for the support of the family of a deceased husband for six months from the date of death and, if a final account has not been allowed, may at any time during the second six months make an additional allowance for that period. After payment of expenses the widow is entitled to $50,000 and one-half the remainder, and the rest is distributed among heirs as with real property. A surviving husband receives $50,000 and one-half the remainder of the personal property, and the rest is distributed among heirs in the same way real estate descends.

When a married person dies without a will leaving a widow or widower and issue, the real estate is subject to dower or curtesy then goes to the children or their descendants in equal shares. One-half the· personal property goes to the surviving spouse and the remainder is distributed among the issue in the same way real estate descends.

South Carolina If a married man or woman dies with children or descendants, the spouse gets one-third of the entire estate, the children two-thirds divided equally. If there is only one child, the widow or widower gets half, and the child gets the other half. If parents, brothers, sisters, or their descendants survive (where there are no children), the wife or husband takes one-half, the other half goes equally to the parents, brothers, sisters. Nieces and nephews take their deceased parent's share. If only parents survive, husband or wife takes half and the balance goes to mother and father or survivor. If only brothers and sisters survive, the widow or widower takes half and the rest is divided equally among the brothers and sisters. Nieces and nephews take their deceased parent's share. If neither parents nor whole brothers or sisters survive, half goes to the husband or wife, the rest to half-brothers and half-sisters, divided equally. If there are no surviving parents, brothers, sisters, their descendants, half-brothers, half-sisters, or lineal ancestors, the entire estate goes to the husband or wife.

South Dakota A surviving widow or widower takes
half, and one child takes the other half. When there
is more than one child, the surviving spouse gets one-
third, the children two-thirds divided equally among
them.

Tennessee The surviving husband or wife gets
dower and all personal property. When there are
children, the widow or widower takes dower and a
share equal to child's personal property.

Texas In this community property state a sole surviving husband or wife gets all the separate and
community property. If there are children, the widow
or widower receives one-half of the community property plus a life interest in one-third of the real estate
owned separately and one-third of the personal
property.

Utah A surviving spouse takes one-half if decedent
left one child or issue of one deceased child, one-
third if decedent left more than one child, all of the
first $100,000 and one-half of excess if decedent left
no issue, but left parent, brother, sister, children, or
grandchildren.

Vermont When there is only a surviving spouse, he
or she gets dower and one-third personal property or
all property to $8,000 and half of the residue of the
estate. If there are children, the husband or wife gets
dower and one-third of the personal property, the children getting two-thirds of the personal property. Upon
the death of surviving parent real estate goes to children equally.

Virginia When there are no children, the widow or
widower gets dower and all personal property. When
there are children, the spouse receives dower and one-
third of the personal property, two-thirds being divided
equally among the children. Upon the death of the surviving parent real estate goes to the children equally.

Washington   This is a community property state.

When there are no children or parents, the surviving spouse takes all the community and separate property. When there are children, the surviving widow or widower receives three-fourths of the community property and one-half of the separate property.

West Virginia   Real estate is divided equally among the children, subject to the surviving husband's or wife's life interest. Other property is divided one-third to husband or wife, two-thirds to the child or children equally divided. If there are no children or descendants, the entire estate goes to the surviving spouse. If there are no surviving spouse, children, or descendants, the estate is equally divided among living parents. If no parents survive, the estate is equally divided among brothers and sisters and their descendants.

Wisconsin   If the intestate is survived by spouse only, the surviving widow or widower takes all the property. If there is issue, the widow or widower takes (a) one-half of the personal property if there is one child and one-third of the personal property in other cases and (b) all the rest of the personal property up to $10,000 if the decedent left no issue by a previous marriage. Any remainder over $10,000 goes to the issue in equal shares per stirpes. As to real property issue takes all, subject to spouse's dower, curtesy, and homestead rights, in equal shares per stirpes. If there are children but no spouse, all the property goes to the issue in equal shares per stirpes. If there are parents but neither spouse nor issue, all the property goes to the parents or parent. If there are only brothers and sisters, all the property goes to the decedent's brothers and sisters and their issue in equal shares per stirpes.

Wyoming   If there is a child or children, the surviving spouse takes half of the estate, the children the balance. If there is no surviving child or issue of such child but there are a surviving parent, brother, sister, or descendant of deceased brother or sister, the surviving spouse gets property up to the value of $20,000 as well as three-fourths of the excess, and the balance goes to the parents, brothers, and sisters equally. If the deceased has no such relatives, surviving spouse gets entire estate.

CHAPTER 4

WHO CAN MAKE A WILL

To make a valid will you must have what the law calls "testamentary capacity." Translated into modern English this means that you meet the statutory age requirements of your particular state, are mentally competent at the time you make the will, and are subjected to neither fraud nor undue influence.

Here are the minimum age requirements for executing a will.

Alabama Twenty-one for real estate, eighteen for personal property.

Alaska Twenty-one for both real and personal property.

Arizona Twenty-one for both real and personal property, anyone who is or was lawfully married, a member of the U. S. Armed forces if eighteen or more.

Arkansas Anyone over eighteen, or a married woman.

California Anyone over eighteen.

Colorado Anyone over eighteen.

Connecticut Anyone over eighteen.

Delaware Anyone over eighteen.

District of Columbia Males over twenty-one, females over eighteen.

Florida Anyone eighteen or over.

Georgia Anyone over fourteen.

Hawaii Anyone over twenty.

45

Idaho Anyone over eighteen.

Illinois Anyone over eighteen.

Indiana Anyone over twenty-one or who is in the Armed Forces or Merchant Marine.

Iowa Anyone over twenty-one.

Kansas Anyone over twenty-one.

Kentucky Anyone over eighteen.

Louisiana Anyone over sixteen.

Maine Anyone over twenty-one, or a married person, widow, or widower of any age.

Maryland Anyone over eighteen.

Massachusetts Anyone over twenty-one or a married woman.

Michigan Anyone over twenty-one.

Minnesota Anyone over twenty-one.

Mississippi Anyone over twenty-one.

Missouri Anyone over eighteen.

Montana Anyone over eighteen.

Nebraska Anyone over twenty-one.

Nevada Anyone over eighteen.

New Hampshire Anyone eighteen or over; if lawfully married, at any age.

New Jersey Anyone over twenty-one, eighteen for those in active military service.

New Mexico Anyone over twenty-one.

New York Anyone over eighteen.

North Carolina Anyone over twenty-one; if married, over eighteen.

North Dakota Anyone over eighteen.

Ohio Anyone over eighteen.

Oklahoma Anyone over eighteen.

Oregon Anyone over twenty-one.

Pennsylvania Anyone over twenty-one, eighteen for those in the Armed Forces or Merchant Marine.

Rhode Island Anyone over twenty-one, those eight-

een or more may dispose of personal property by
will.

South Carolina Anyone over twenty-one or over
eighteen and married.

South Dakota Anyone over eighteen.

Tennessee Anyone over eighteen.

Texas Anyone over eighteen or who has been lawfully married; anyone, regardless of age, who is in the
Armed Forces or Maritime Service.

Utah Anyone over eighteen.

Vermont Anyone over twenty-one.

Virginia Anyone over twenty-one, those over eighteen may dispose of personal property.

Washington Anyone over twenty-one, anyone eighteen or over who is married or is in the Armed Forces
or Merchant Marine.

West Virginia Anyone over twenty-one.

Wisconsin Anyone over twenty-one, or any married
woman over eighteen, or anyone in the Armed Forces.

Wyoming Anyone over twenty-one.

For your will to hold up in court you must have a
certain mental capacity. You do not have to be a genius
or have even average intelligence. All the law requires
is that you understand the nature and consequences of
preparing a will. Specifically, you must understand in
general terms the nature and extent of the property
you own and the persons who normally would be entitled to receive it. As one court put it, you can leave
a valid will even though the terms are "as eccentric,
as injudicious, or as unjust as caprice, frivolity, or re-
venge can dictate." In other words, you can leave your
kinfolk as much or as little as you wish just as long as
you realize that you do have a family that normally
would be the object of your bounty.

To the general rule that practically anyone can make

a will, there are certain exceptions. An idiot or imbecile in the psychiatric or medical sense may lack the capacity to understand the nature of the will making process, but the fact that one is mentally inferior does not necessarily imply incapacity to make a simple will.

It is otherwise with paranoics. A paranoic is one afflicted with delusions of persecution and extreme jealousy. He may feel, for example, that a son is out to poison him when there is no evidence to support such a view. The paranoic could attempt to cut off the son in the will even though he had been loyal, dedicated, and affectionate. When offered for probate, the will of a paranoic supported by competent psychiatric evidence will be refused on the ground that the testator lacked testamentary capacity.

The mere fact of undergoing psychiatric treatment does not necessarily mean a lack of the requisite mental capacity to prepare a will. Many people at one time or another are emotionally disturbed or neurotic and may require such crutches as sleeping potions, tranquilizers, drugs, and alcohol. Of course, no lawyer should prepare a will where there is strong evidence that the testator is psychotic or otherwise mentally unsound. However, the very concept of insanity is itself ambiguous. A psychiatrist will define it one way, a lawyer another, a layman still another way. Not all persons suffering from delusions of persecution are confined to mental institutions. Nor are all schizophrenics or manic depressives. Many walk the streets, able to function reasonably well in their jobs.

Mere eccentricities do not normally constitute testamentary incapacity. You can still execute a valid will even if you prefer the company of cats to people or denounce the President of the United States as a rogue and scoundrel. You can dress as outrageously as you please and still be normal enough to write a will.

You might even have false beliefs about members of your family, but if there is the slightest evidence for your belief, even if false, your will will be upheld. You may be convinced, for example, that one of your sons is not really yours and disinherit him from your will because in the course of a violent domestic quarrel your wife taunted you with her infidelity and cast doubt on the legitimacy of the child.

In the matter of will-making the law is rather tolerant. You can believe in any or all religions or be a convinced atheist or agnostic. You can believe in spiritualism, Christian Science, or Seventh Day Adventism, and there will be no one to say you nay. You can live the life of a libertine, enjoying wine, women, and song, or you can spend your days in prayer and contemplation. You can even be convicted of theft, fraud, or all sorts of skullduggery and spend years in prison, and still not forfeit your right to leave a will.

Today even blind, illiterate, and deaf and dumb testators may have wills prepared for them, provided proper precautions are observed. In the case of a blind person, for example, there should be affidavits from witnesses that the will was read by the testator and understood by him to be his act. In the case of a person who can neither read nor write, there should be similar statements from disinterested witnesses. As to deaf mutes, there is no legal presumption that they lack testamentary capacity.

Fraud invalidates a will. If a blind testator is willfully deceived by the beneficiary as to the contents of the document, the will is void, and the property passes under the laws of intestacy. Fortunately, instances of deception in the case of wills are relatively rare.

What constitutes undue influence is in general difficult to determine and must be judged from the facts of a particular case. Undue influence is any unusual pres-

sure or persuasion by which one person is compelled
to do some act which will benefit the person doing the
pressing or persuading. If you leave everything to your
mistress to the exclusion of your children, the court
may say you acted under undue influence and upset
the will. The mere fact that a will is unjust in its provisions does not necessarily mean that undue influence
was exerted.

Four elements are necessary to establish undue influence. They are:

1. A testator who is subject to undue influence.
2. An opportunity to use it.
3. A willingness to use it.
4. A result which destroys the free agency of the
testator.

Take the case of Jones. Immediately after he under-
went brain surgery, Mrs. Jones persuaded him to make
a will leaving all his property to her, completely ig-
noring his dependent children by a previous marriage.
Such a will might be upset on the ground of undue influence since the husband was too weak to resist the
wife's pressure.

Not all special pleading is considered undue influence. A son urges his mother to make a will in his behalf, which she later does. Such a will would not be
considered unduly influenced since a son or daughter
has a right to urge a parent to make a will in his favor.
If the only effect of such prompting is to arouse the
mother's affection or appeal to a parent's sense of duty,
it would be unobjectionable.

Threats of violence or of litigation among the children or criminal prosecution of the testator may all
constitute undue influence. Mere advice and persuasion
do not. Proving undue influence is extremely difficult.
Less than seven percent of those seeking to upset a will
on this ground are successful.

CHAPTER 5

SHOULD YOU WRITE YOUR OWN WILL?

There is compelling logic for leaving a will, but the tragic fact is that three out of every four persons die without ever having written one.

Fear and anxiety about death cause some people to delay until too late. The average person's tendency to identify wills with death, leads him to the odd notion that postponing the will may delay his demise. In fact, experience suggests that many testators outlive the very lawyers who prepared their wills. Others procrastinate because they think themselves too young to bother about wills, or too healthy. Writing a will is not a matter of age or health. The young die as well as the old, and rain falls on the healthy as well as on the lame and the halt.

Many people know so little about the will-making process that they simply do not know where to take the first step. They are embarrassed about their ignorance, apprehensive about consulting a lawyer, and even more hesitant about doing the job themselves. They have a vague feeling that somehow or other the state will distribute their property fairly.

People too busy with their jobs, business, or careers find it easy to delay. They are so pre-occupied making money or with extra-curricular activities that they just cannot find the time—or pretend they cannot—to leave intelligent directions about the disposition of their property.

Writing a will is often deferred because of misconceptions. Some believe that a will cannot be changed or that there must first be a complete inventory of the estate. Neither statement is true. Since a will takes effect only on death, you can change it as often as you like. Nor do you need even a partial inventory of your estate. You can leave your property in its entirety or in whatever fractional portions you desire without naming a single piece of either personal or real estate. For example, a simple statement in the residuary clause that you "give, bequeath and devise *all* my estate, real and personal to my wife," can be ample to carry out your purpose.

Another popular misconception is that you cannot sell or otherwise dispose of property after you have bequeathed it in a will. You can. Since a will takes effect only upon death, only what is left at the time of death is distributed. In short, after you write a will you may still dispose of your property any way you like. You can trade your securities or sell your real estate with no restrictions.

Nor is it necessary that you get your business in good shape or pay off all your debts before you write a will. The worse shape your business is in, the more urgent the need for a will. After you are gone, your debts will be paid if there are sufficient assets; if your debts exceed your assets, there will be nothing to distribute anyway.

The terms of your will need not be discussed with your spouse, children, or any other beneficiary of your largess. Only you need know the contents of your will, and your attorney if you consult one. Nor is it necessary or even desirable, as many people think, to deposit the will in the probate court while you still live. While many courts do allow for such safe-keeping, you can deposit your will any place you please: in your desk, your safe deposit box, or with your child or spouse. Even so, there is nothing to prevent you from changing your will as often as circumstances warrant. It is your *last* will that counts, not the first, second, or third.

When you are finally convinced you should have a will, you can do it one of two ways: write it yourself or have an experienced attorney write it up for you.

If you have average intelligence, can follow simple directions, and are not concerned with complicated wills, trust agreements, or tax problems, there is no reason why you cannot write a simple will that is binding and effective.

First, a few cautions. Do not write in pencil; a will should be written in ink or typed. Be sure it is letter perfect; do not make any corrections on the will itself. If you have made mistakes, do the will over and over until it is letter perfect. You should not erase, cross out words, or correct anything on the will itself. If you do, it may be declared invalid and your property will pass as if you had not written a will.

Below are eight samples of simple wills covering a variety of situations which the average testator or testatrix can handle with relative safety. You could select the form which exactly fits your special situation, copy it exactly, cross out the word or words which do not apply, and have it properly executed as explained later in the chapter. If you do not feel confident about writing your own will, by all means consult an attorney.

Note: It is not necessary to use an actual seal on a will. The word "(SEAL)" is sufficient.

1. Will of childless married person leaving everything to spouse. If spouse fails to survive testator, entire estate goes to someone else:

Last Will and Testament

I, _____ of the city/town of _____, state of _____, do make, publish, and declare this to be my Last Will and Testament, hereby revoking all wills and codicils previously made by me.

First. I hereby direct my Executrix (Executor), hereinafter named, to pay all my just debts and funeral expenses and to have a suitable marker erected at my grave. I direct that I be buried in the _____ cemetery located at _____ in the aforementioned city/town.

Second, I give, devise, and bequeath all the rest and residue of my estate, real and personal, to my wife (husband) _____.

Third. If my said wife (husband) fails to survive me, I give my entire estate, real and personal, to:

NAME	ADDRESS		
_____	_____		
	Street	City	State

Fourth. I hereby appoint my wife (husband) Executrix (Executor) of my estate. If she (he) does not survive me, then I appoint _____ as my Executor.

Fifth. I direct that my Executrix or Executor, as the case may be, shall be excused from furnishing bond.

IN TESTIMONY WHEREOF, I subscribe my name and affix my seal, this _____ day of _____ in the year _____.

      (sign here) _____(SEAL)

Signed, sealed, published, and declared by the within named Testator (Testatrix) in the presence of us who at his (her) request, in his (her) presence, and in the presence of each other, hereunto subscribe our names as witnesses.

	NAME	ADDRESS		
(1)	_____	_____		
(2)	_____	_____		
(3)	_____	_____		
		Street	City	State

2. Will of married person with children leaving everything to spouse. If spouse does not survive, everything goes to children in equal shares:

Last Will and Testament

I, _____ of the city/town of _____,
state of _____, do make, publish, and declare this
to be my Last Will and Testament, hereby revoking all wills
and codicils previously made by me.

First. I hereby direct my Executrix (Executor), hereinafter named, to pay all my just debts and funeral expenses and
to have a suitable marker erected at my grave. I direct that
I be buried in the _____ cemetery located
at _____ in the aforementioned city/town.

Second. I give, devise, and bequeath all the rest and residue of my estate, real and personal, to my wife (husband)

_____.

Third. If my said wife (husband) does not survive me, I
give, devise, and bequeath all the rest and residue of my
estate to my children in equal shares, per stirpes, to be
theirs absolutely and forever, provided that the share of
any child who has died leaving no issue shall be divided
among my surviving children in equal shares, per stirpes.

Fourth. I hereby appoint my wife (husband) Executrix
(Executor) of my estate. If she (he) does not survive me,
then I appoint _____ as my Executor.

Fifth. I direct that my Executrix or Executor, as the case
may be, shall be excused from furnishing bond.

IN TESTIMONY WHEREOF, I subscribe my name and
affix my seal, this ____ day of _____ in the year ____.
(sign here) _____(SEAL)

Signed, sealed, published, and declared by the within
named Testator (Testatrix) in the presence of us who at his
(her) request, in his (her) presence, and in the presence of
each other, hereunto subscribe our names as witnesses.

NAME	ADDRESS
(1) _____	_____
(2) _____	_____
(3) _____	_____
	Street City State

3. Will of childless married person leaving major portion
of estate to spouse and certain specific bequests to others:

Last Will and Testament

I, _____ of the city/town of _____, state of _____, do make, publish, and declare this to be my Last Will and Testament, hereby revoking all wills and codicils previously made by me.

First. I hereby direct my Executrix (Executor), hereinafter named, to pay all my just debts and funeral expenses and to have a suitable marker erected at my grave. I direct that I be buried in the _____ cemetery located at _____ in the aforementioned city/town.

Second. I give and bequeath the following sums of money to each of the herein named persons:

$_____	_____
Amount	Name
	_____
	Address
$_____	_____
Amount	Name
	_____
	Address
$_____	_____
Amount	Name
	_____
	Address

Third. I give, devise, and bequeath all the rest and residue of my estate, real and personal, to my wife (husband)

_____.

Fourth. If my said wife (husband) does not survive me then all the rest and residue of my estate is to go to:

NAME	ADDRESS		
_____	_____		
	Street	City	State

Fifth. I hereby appoint my wife (husband) Executrix (Executor) of my estate. If she (he) does not survive me, then I appoint _____ as my Executor.

Sixth. I direct that by Executrix or Executor, as the case may be, shall be excused from furnishing bond.

IN TESTIMONY WHEREOF, I subscribe my name and affix my seal, this _____ day of _____ in the year _____.

(sign here) _____ (SEAL)

Signed, sealed, published, and declared by the within named Testator (Testatrix) in the presence of us who at his (her) request, in his (her) presence, and in the presence of each other, hereunto subscribe our names as witnesses.

NAME	ADDRESS
(1) _____	_____
(2) _____	_____
(3) _____	_____
	Street City State

4. Will of widow or widower leaving estate to children in equal shares:

LAST WILL AND TESTAMENT

I, _____ of the city/town of _____, state of _____, do make, publish, and declare this to be my Last Will and Testament, hereby revoking all wills and codicils previously made by me.

First. I hereby direct my Executrix (Executor), hereinafter named, to pay all my just debts and funeral expenses and to have a suitable marker erected at my grave. I direct that I be buried in the _____ cemetery located at _____ in the aforementioned city/town.

Second. I give, devise, and bequeath all the rest and residue of my estate, real and personal, to my children in equal shares, per stirpes, to be theirs absolutely and forever, provided that the share of any child who has died leaving no issue shall be divided among my surviving children in equal shares, per stirpes.

Third. I hereby appoint _____ Executrix (Executor) of my estate. If she (he) does not survive me, then I appoint _____ as my Executor.

Fourth. I direct that my Executrix or Executor, as the case may be, shall be excused from furnishing bond.

IN TESTIMONY WHEREOF, I subscribe my name and affix my seal, this _____ day of _____ in the year _____.

(sign here) _____ (SEAL)

Signed, sealed, published, and declared by the within named Testator (Testatrix) in the presence of us who at his (her) request, in his (her) presence, and in the presence of each other, hereunto subscribe our names as witnesses.

	NAME	ADDRESS
(1)	_____	_____
(2)	_____	_____
(3)	_____	_____
		Street City State

5. Will of childless person leaving everything to parents or survivor of them:

LAST WILL AND TESTAMENT

I, _____ of the city/town of _____, state of _____, do make, publish, and declare this to be my Last Will and Testament, hereby revoking all wills and codicils previously made by me.

First. I hereby direct my Executrix (Executor), hereinafter named, to pay all my just debts and funeral expenses and to have a suitable marker erected at my grave. I direct that I be buried in the _____ cemetery located at _____ in the aforementioned city/town.

Second. I give, devise, and bequeath all the rest and residue of my estate, real and personal, to my parents in equal shares, or to the survivor of them. If my said parents do not survive me, then my entire estate, real and personal, is to go to:

NAME	ADDRESS
_____	_____
	Street City State

Third. I hereby appoint _____ Executrix (Executor) of my estate. If she (he) does not survive me, then I appoint _____ as my Executor.

Fourth. I direct that by Executrix or Executor, as the case may be, shall be excused from furnishing bond.

IN TESTIMONY WHEREOF, I subscribe my name and affix my seal, this ____ day of _____ in the year ____.

(sign here) _____ (SEAL)

Signed, sealed, published, and declared by the within named Testator (Testatrix) in the presence of us who at his (her) request, in his (her) presence, and in the presence of each other, hereunto subscribe our names as witnesses.

NAME	ADDRESS
(1) _____	_____
(2) _____	_____
(3) _____	_____
	Street City State

6. Will of childless person leaving everything to brothers and sisters in equal shares:

LAST WILL AND TESTAMENT

I, _____ of the city/town of _____, state of _____, do make, publish, and declare this to be my Last Will and Testament, hereby revoking all wills and codicils previously made by me.

First. I hereby direct my Executrix (Executor), hereinafter named, to pay all my just debts and funeral expenses and to have a suitable marker erected at my grave. I direct that I be buried in the _____ cemetery located at _____ in the aforementioned city/town.

Second. I give, devise, and bequeath all the rest and residue of my estate, real and personal, to my brothers and sisters in equal shares, or to the survivor of them.

Third. The share of any brother or sister who shall not survive me shall go to such brother or sister's issue in equal shares, per stirpes. If such brother or sister dies leaving no issue, the share designated above as being for such brother or sister shall be divided among the surviving beneficiaries in equal shares, per stirpes.

Fourth. I hereby appoint _____ Executrix (Executor) of my estate. If she (he) does not survive me, then I appoint _____ as my Executor.

Fifth. I direct that my Executrix or Executor, as the case may be, shall be excused from furnishing bond.

IN TESTIMONY WHEREOF, I subscribe my name and affix my seal, this _____ day of _____ in the year _____.

(sign here) _____ (SEAL)

Signed, sealed, published, and declared by the within

named Testator (Testatrix) in the presence of us who at his
(her) request, in his (her) presence, and in the presence of
each other, hereunto subscribe our names as witnesses.

NAME	ADDRESS
(1) _____	_____
(2) _____	_____
(3) _____	_____
	Street City State

7. Will of childless person leaving everything to one or
more persons:

LAST WILL AND TESTAMENT

I, _____ of the city/town of _____,
state of _____, do make, publish, and declare this
to be my Last Will and Testament, hereby revoking all wills
and codicils previously made by me.

First. I hereby direct my Executrix (Executor), hereinafter named, to pay all my just debts and funeral expenses and
to have a suitable marker erected at my grave. I direct that
I be buried in the _____ cemetery located
at _____ in the aforementioned city/town.

Second. I give, devise, and bequeath all the rest and residue of my estate to the following persons in equal shares:

NAME	ADDRESS
_____	_____
_____	_____
	Street City State

Third. The share of any person above named who shall
not survive me shall go to such person's issue in equal
shares, per stirpes. If such person has died leaving no issue,
the share designated above as being for such person shall
go to the survivor of the two beneficiaries named above.

Fourth. I hereby appoint _____ Executrix
(Executor) of my estate. If she (he) does not survive me,
then I appoint _____ as my Executor.

Fifth. I direct that my Executrix or Executor, as the case
may be, shall be excused from furnishing bond.

IN TESTIMONY WHEREOF, I subscribe my name and

affix my seal, this _____ day of _____ in the year _____.
(sign here) _____(SEAL)

Signed, sealed, published, and declared by the within named Testator (Testatrix) in the presence of us who at his (her) request, in his (her) presence, and in the presence of each other, hereunto subscribe our names as witnesses.

NAME	ADDRESS
(1) _____	_____
(2) _____	_____
(3) _____	_____
	Street City State

8. Will of person with children leaving part or all of estate to children in unequal shares:

LAST WILL AND TESTAMENT

I, _____ of the city/town of _____, state of _____, do make, publish, and declare this to be my Last Will and Testament, hereby revoking all wills and codicils previously made by me.

First. I hereby direct my Executrix (Executor), hereinafter named, to pay all my just debts and funeral expenses and to have a suitable marker erected at my grave. I direct that I be buried in the _____ cemetery located at _____ in the aforementioned city/town.

Second. I give and bequeath the sum of $_____ to my son (daughter) _____.

Third. I give, bequeath, and devise all the rest and residue of my estate to my other children in equal shares.

Fourth. I hereby appoint _____ Executrix (Executor) of my estate. If she (he) does not survive me, then I appoint _____ as my Executor.

Fifth. I direct that my Executrix or Executor, as the case may be, shall be excused from furnishing bond.

IN TESTIMONY WHEREOF, I subscribe my name and affix my seal, this _____ day of _____ in the year _____.
(sign here) _____(SEAL)

Signed, sealed, published, and declared by the within named Testator (Testatrix) in the presence of us who at his (her) request, in his (her) presence, and in the presence of each other, hereunto subscribe our names as witnesses.

NAME	ADDRESS
(1) _____	_____
(2) _____	_____
(3) _____	_____
	Street City State

If you have written your own will using one of the forms in this chapter as a guide—and so saved the $100–$150 fee lawyers normally charge for a simply drawn will—what do you do next?

Have the will properly witnessed and signed. Connecticut, Georgia, Louisiana, Maine, Massachusetts, New Hampshire, South Carolina, and Vermont require three witnesses to a will. All the remaining states, including the District of Columbia, require two. However, it is wise to have the added safety of three witnesses even in those states which require only two. A will signed by the testator but not properly witnessed by the number required in a particular state is invalid, and the estate will be distributed as if the testator had left no will.

Choose your witnesses carefully. They are important if any question later arises about the validity of the will or the competency of the testator. They will be the ones to testify if the will is contested after your death, whether you write the will yourself or have it drawn by your attorney.

In choosing your witnesses exercise some important cautions:

Don't use a beneficiary under your will. He may have to forfeit his gift under the will if he helps to probate it.

Don't use someone very close to the beneficiary. Suspicion may be aroused that he unduly influenced you.

Don't choose a witness older than yourself. You run the risk that he may die before you do and put your estate to the trouble and experience of proving the deceased witness's handwriting.

Don't choose an out of state witness or one who does a great deal of traveling. Your executor may have trouble finding him when he is needed or have the added expense of bringing him in from another state.

Don't choose a timid or ignorant witness. You may make it difficult for your executor when it comes to proving your competency in case of a contest.

Your witnesses should not only be younger than you, but well established members of the community in which you live. They can be your next door neighbors. They can be professional or business friends or acquaintances, and the longer they have known you the better. Above all, they should be disinterested in the content of the will and have a reputation in the community for unquestioned integrity.

Witnesses to a will don't have to appear in court unless the will is contested after the testator's death.

After you have written your will and chosen your three witnesses, the next step is to get in touch with each of them and arrange for a time and place for the signing and witnessing of the will.

The procedure is a simple one. Announce to all three witnesses that the document you hold in your hand is your last will and testament and that you would like them to witness it. You do not have to reveal the contents of the will, the names of the beneficiaries, or anything else about the document.

After the witnesses have agreed to serve, you sign the will in their presence—in ink—after which each witness signs his or her name in ink, including his or her address. Each witness should observe not only the testator or testatrix sign, but all should watch each other sign; no witness should leave the room until all the witnesses have signed.

One final caution, your signature and those of your witnesses should be on the same page. If your will is longer than one page, initial each page on the left hand margin of your will. Each page should be numbered and, if the will contains more than one page, it should be clipped or stapled together. With the completion of the ceremony, your will is now properly executed.

Chapter 6

WHAT YOU SHOULD KNOW
ABOUT EXECUTORS

The choice of an executor is one of the most important decisions you will ever be called upon to make. Consider some of the duties of an executor or, if you leave no will, an administrator. Among other things he must:

1. Locate your will.

2. Carry out the funeral arrangements made in the will.

3. Collect the personal effects and preserve them from waste.

4. Probate the will and be appointed executor.

5. Keep accurate records of all estate transactions.

6. Open the safe deposit box, if any.

7. Assume control over all personal property.

8. Do whatever is necessary to liquidate or to carry on the business.

9. Determine the debts due the estate and see that they are paid.

10. Determine and collect all assets due the estate.

11. Arrange for the collection of all insurance payable to the estate.

12. Make arrangements for the transfer of all stocks, bonds, and other securities from the name of the decedent to that of the executor.

13. Pay all taxes and other expenses of the estate.

14. Have all property, real and personal, appraised for tax purposes.

15. Defend the estate against any suits.

16. Pay all legacies to those named in the will.

17. Submit a final accounting to the court.

Obviously, this is a substantial job requiring skill, patience, experience, judgment, and intelligence. A common practice is to name the surviving spouse as executor or executrix. This is done as a compliment to the surviving spouse and to save on the executor's commission.

However, in ninety-nine cases out of a hundred your spouse will still have to employ counsel to actually administer the estate whether it is a small one of $10,000 or less, a medium-sized one of $60,000, or a substantial one of $100,000 or more. An attorney's charge to handle the estate will depend on its size, his reputation and experience, and the amount of time involved. The usual arrangement is to divide the executor's commission, which is set by law, on a fifty-fifty basis. Some attorneys will ask more, some less. In all cases there should be a clear understanding as to the exact division since the attorney will be doing all the work.

What is true for a surviving spouse is equally true for a trusted friend who has agreed to serve as executor. Given the best will in the world, the friend will also require a lawyer's expert assistance in the actual management of the estate. Here, too, the friend will share the commission with the attorney he engages.

A good practice, if you have confidence in your attorney and he is familiar with both your family and your holdings, is to name him in the will as co-executor along with your spouse. If the estate is $60,000 or more, it is sound to name both your attorney and a trust company as co-executors. They will usually divide the commission between them according to who does most of the work.

The reasons for including a trust company for a substantial estate are persuasive. In the first place, it is the business of a trust company to handle estates just as it may be the testator's business to practice medicine or dentistry. Second, most of the trust companies have financial responsibility which protects against unsatisfactory results. Third, a trust company is a corporation with perpetual existence and there is never any need to appoint a new executor if the individual assigned to handle your particular estate resigns or dies.

Fourth, the average trust company has been in business for many years and has accumulated a vast amount of invaluable experience. It employs experts in stocks and bonds, real estate, and various business enterprises. It specializes in trusts where income goes to beneficiaries but not principal. A generally conservative approach is an added safeguard against speculative excesses or the wasting of the estate's assets and can be especially important in the case of a widow or child who requires income without responsibility.

This does not mean that all trust companies are equally good. They are not. Some are dull and stodgy; some have unimpressive records in the investing of securities or in the handling of estates. But by and large the record of the better trust companies is apt to be favorable, which is why more and more of them are named co-executors of substantial estates.

A good plan, if you wish to preserve a going business, is to name as co-executor someone familiar with it. A trust company can run a business but may have to employ an outside expert. If you operate a manufacturing plant, for example, you may wish to consider a close business associate or trusted advisor who is thoroughly familiar with company operations.

Although you name an executor or co-executor of your will, you cannot compel an individual or a trust company to serve. The company is in the business of making money and may refuse to handle an estate which appears unprofitable. If you wish to name a trust company as co-executor, arrange an interview with the trust officer and discuss with him in confidence the nature of your estate together with its assets and liabilities. After being given the facts he may decide that your estate is not the kind his company would handle. If so, you will know where you stand and can make other arrangements.

Also worth remembering is that, unless you name your own attorney as executor or co-executor of your will, the executor is perfectly free to choose his or her own counsel.

Finally, an executor—whether a surviving spouse, friend, attorney, or trust company—is entitled to a commission for the work done. That fee or commission varies from state to state and is set by law. Listed here by states are the commissions allowed executors and administrators.

Alabama   Not in excess of two and a half percent on receipts and two and a half percent on disbursements. Also actual expenses including bond premiums and just compensation for extraordinary services. For selling lands for division, two and a half percent but not more than $100 unless lands are sold under will.

Alaska   Seven percent on all up to $1,000, five percent on excess to $2,000, four percent on excess to $4,000, two percent on excess over $4,000. Reasonable compensation may be allowed for extraordinary services.

Arizona   Seven percent on first $1,000, five percent on all above that sum and not over $10,000, four percent on all above that. Allowance made for extraordinary services.

Arkansas   Ten percent of first $1,000, five percent of next $4,000, and three percent of balance of value of personal property; additional compensation may be allowed for extraordinary services. Compensation for legal services is based on total market value of estate: five percent of first $5,000, four percent of next $20,000, three percent of next $75,000, two and three-fourths percent of next $300,000, two and a half percent of next $600,000, and two percent of balance.

California Seven percent on first $1,000, four percent on next $9,000, three percent on next $40,000, two percent on next $100,000, one and one-fourth percent on next $350,000, and one percent on all over $500,000. Court may allow additional compensation for extraordinary services.

Colorado Six percent where estate is less than $25,000, four percent on next $75,000, three percent on balance. Court may allow additional compensation for extraordinary services.

Connecticut No statutory rate.

Delaware Not more than ten percent.

District of Columbia From one percent to ten percent.

Florida Six percent on first $1,000, four percent on excess to $5,000, two and one-half percent on excess over $5,000.

Georgia Two and one-half percent on money received and two and one-half percent on money paid out.

Hawaii On moneys received or income seven percent on first $5,000 and five percent on all over $5,000, allowance being made on each accounting. On principal of estate five percent on first $1,000, four percent on next $9,000, three percent on next $10,000, two percent for all over $20,000.

Idaho Five percent on first $1,000, four percent on excess to $10,000, three percent on balance.

Illinois Reasonable compensation, no stated rate.

Indiana   Reasonable compensation, no stated rate.

Iowa   Six percent on first $1,000, four percent on the excess up to $5,000, two percent on the excess over $5,000. Extra compensation provided for extraordinary services and expenses.

Kansas   Reasonable compensation and expenses.

Kentucky   Compensation may not exceed five percent of the value of the personal estate plus five percent of the income. Additional compensation allowed for services in connection with real estate and inheritance taxes.

Louisiana   Two and one-half percent of the value of the estate.

Maine   Five percent on amount of personal assets and reasonable sum for necessary legal counsel. May receive additional one percent of principal of trust fund; also commission of five percent allowed at termination of trust.

Maryland   Ten percent on first $20,000 and four percent on balance over $20,000.

Massachusetts   No fixed rate but commission of three percent of estate up to $500,000 and one percent of balance is considered not unreasonable.

Michigan   Five percent of first $1,000, two and one-half percent on excess to $5,000, two percent on remainder.

Minnesota   Necessary expenses and reasonable compensation for services.

Mississippi   Not more than seven percent of entire estate.

Missouri   Not stated.

Montana   Seven percent on first $1,000, five percent on excess to $10,000, four percent on excess to $20,000, two percent on excess over $20,000.

Nebraska   Five percent on first $1,000, two and one-half percent on next $4,000, and two percent on all over $5,000. Additional allowances may be made for extraordinary services.

Nevada Six percent on first $1,000, four percent on next $4,000, two percent on excess over $5,000. Attorneys' fees are fixed and allowed by court.

New Hampshire Not stated.

New Jersey Five percent on first $100,000 and five percent on excess.

New Mexico Ten percent on first $3,000 and five percent on excess. Compensation on real estate is set by court.

New York For receiving and paying out first $10,000, four percent; for receiving and paying out next $290,000, two and one-half percent; all above $300,000, two percent. If gross estate is $100,000 or more, each co-executor or administrator is entitled to full commission. For collecting rents or managing property personal representative is allowed five percent of gross rents in addition to commission.

North Carolina Five percent of receipts and expenditures.

North Dakota Five percent of first $1,000 of assets, three percent of next $5,000, two percent of next $4,000, and two percent of excess.

Ohio Six percent on the first $1,000, four percent on the next $4,000, and two percent of the remainder.

Oklahoma Five percent on first $1,000, four percent on next $4,000, two and one-half percent on excess over $5,000.

Oregon First $1,000, seven percent; between $1,000 and $10,000, four percent; between $10,000 and $50,000, three percent; above $50,000, two percent.

Pennsylvania No statute. Practice is to allow five percent on small estates and three percent on large estates.

Rhode Island At discretion of court.

South Carolina Two and one-half percent on appraised value.

South Dakota On the first $1,000, five percent; between $1,000 and $5,000, four percent; all over $5,000, two and one-half percent.

Tennessee Determined by court on basis of services performed.

Texas Five percent of all money received and five percent of all money paid in cash. Commission not to exceed more than five percent of gross fair market value of estate.

Utah Five percent on first $1,000, four percent on excess to $5,000, three percent on excess to $100,000, one percent on excess over $100,000.

Vermont Four dollars a day while attending duties of office; probate court may allow further compensation in cases of unusual difficulty and responsibility.

Virginia Usually five percent but may be increased or decreased.

Washington Determined by court.

West Virginia Five percent.

Wisconsin Five percent on first $1,000, one percent on next $19,000, two percent on all above $20,000; also, $10 per day for actual time required as well as allowances for extraordinary services.

Wyoming On first $1,000, ten percent; from $1,000 to $5,000, five percent; between $5,000 and $20,000, three percent; for amounts over $20,000, two percent.

Note: The fees for executors and administrators do not include compensation of trustees who distribute income to beneficiaries. These vary by states on a graduated scale.

Chapter 7

WHAT TO LEAVE AND HOW TO LEAVE IT

The best drawn will may be worthless unless it can be located. Unhappily, many wills—especially those drawn by the testator himself—never see the light of day. Some are lost, some stolen, some mislaid, and some are burned up. A will that cannot be found cannot be probated, so your efforts to dispose of your property intelligently could come to naught.

There are various solutions to this vexatious problem. If you write the will yourself, make certain it will be discovered among your other valuable papers—insurance policies, deed to your home, stocks and bonds, title to your automobile, etc. You can do this simply by getting a manilla envelope, marking it "Valuable Papers," and placing your last will and testament in it. Be sure to let someone, your spouse, a relative, a friend, know where your will can be found.

Another possibility is placing your will in a safe deposit box in a bank or trust company. The disadvantage is that a bank will seal your box when it receives notice of your death even if the safe deposit box is jointly held. Your executor would then have to obtain a court order to reopen the box in order to find your will. You could spare him some trouble by providing him the name and address of the bank or trust company where you keep your valuable papers.

73

If your will is written by your lawyer and he is named as your executor or co-executor, you can ask him to give you the original or you can allow him to hold the will for you. If you do not contemplate making any changes and have confidence in your counsel, there is no reason why you should not ask him to retain it. Allowing your attorney to retain your will, however, does not preclude you from changing it or having it rewritten as often as you like.

If you name a trust company as executor, that company will be glad to safeguard your will. Here again there is nothing to prevent you from making a new will any time you please, since it is only your *last* will and testament that is eligible for probate.

What about funeral arrangements? I am dubious about leaving these directions in the will itself, for the reason that a testator is apt to be buried before the will comes to light. A better practice is to leave a written note or memorandum giving detailed instructions with either your spouse, some close relative, or a valued friend.

If you wish to be cremated instead of buried, say so. If you want a gaudy funeral with all the stops out, there is no reason why you cannot humor your wish in a written note. If you desire a modest funeral with few histrionics, a written memorandum is still the way to transmit your instructions. Funeral arrangements should cover other things as well, the name and address of the cemetery in which you are to be buried and the specific plot, the name of the rabbi or minister you prefer to have officiate, and provision for upkeep of the grave (since many cemeteries do not furnish perpetual care). If you have a whimsical turn of mind, you can even design the grave marker with the epitaph for which you would like to be remembered.

Whether you write a simple will yourself or entrust

it to a skilled and experienced attorney, you will need both information and a plan to dispose of your property intelligently. And since lawyers charge by the hour, the more facts you have with you when you consult your attorney, the less he is likely to charge.

1. *Beneficiaries* To begin with list on a blank sheet of paper your possible beneficiaries together with their addresses. Included in the list might be the following:

Spouse
Children
Grandchildren
Brothers
Sisters
Parents
Nieces
Nephews
Other Relatives
Friends
Charities

Then begin a screening process. What, if anything, do you wish to leave to each? Is your spouse to get your entire estate or only a portion? Principal or income? If only a share, how much? What, if anything, will you leave the children? Will they get income or principal? What about a guardian, if the youngsters are under age and you leave them property? Are the children to share and share alike, or are you to give special consideration to those less affluent or ill?

2. *Payment of debts.* What monies do you owe? On a separate sheet of paper list your outstanding obligations, including notes you have signed, mortgages, and possible claims against your estate that should be contested. If such claims are likely to arise, set down the facts about each one. Do you wish your executor to renew any notes for which you are the endorser or

guarantor? Do you wish each legatee to pay the inheritance tax due, if any, or do you want the general estate to pay all necessary taxes? Do you have any preference as to which of your assets are sold in case there is not enough ready cash to pay your debts?

3. *Property that will pass outside your will.* This includes property held jointly by husband and wife with right of survivorship, insurance policies with a named beneficiary, and United States Savings Bonds held in the name of one person and payable on death to another. Any attempt to transfer a pension payable directly during the life of a particular person is usually null and void.

4. *Personal effects.* First to be considered are family heirlooms. An heirloom is any family possession that is handed down from generation to generation. It may be a piece of jewelry such as a diamond ring or a necklace, a work of art such as a portrait of a member of the family, or an original Renoir or Matisse if you are fortunate enough to own one. Do you wish such heirlooms to stay in the family, be given to some specific member, or go into the residuary or general estate?

Under personal effects are listed at least the following:

Automobiles
Clothing
Jewelry
Works of art
Books
Television sets
Stereo equipment and record players
Antiques
Musical instruments
China
Silver
Linens

Tableware
Furniture
House furnishings
Boats

There are several methods of disposing of such personal effects. One is to leave everything to your spouse or to some other specified beneficiary. A second is to earmark certain articles, jewelry, silver, china, and tableware, for example, to specified individuals, naming each article in the will as going to a named person. A third method is to ask your executor to distribute the articles in equal parts by value. A fourth way is to have your executor sell everything, with the money going into the general estate to be divided according to your wishes. A fifth plan is to adopt some compromise among the first four methods.

If the family car is titled in your name and that of your spouse, upon your death the car will automatically pass to your spouse. If the automobile is titled in your own name, you can leave it to your spouse. If your spouse does not drive and there is no one else to give it to, you need not mention the car in your will at all. It will be sold and the proceeds added to the assets of your estate. The same applies to all your other personal effects.

If your spouse is the sole beneficiary, there is no reason why he or she should not have the personal effects to dispose of as desired. The problem arises when there is no surviving spouse but only children or brothers and sisters. Assume, for example, that three children are left. Who is to get what of your personal effects? To earmark certain pieces of jewelry for one child and other pieces to another child may invite more problems than solutions. One child may not like the article left him or think it has less value than a piece left another child. Envy, strife, and bitterness might be

avoided if you instruct your executor to sell all your
personal effects and divide the proceeds in a way you
think most equitable or just.

5. *Family allowances.* A serious, prolonged illness
can drain family resources. Death is expensive. The
settling of an estate can drag on a year or more before
distribution is made. To avoid such hardships most
states make provision for family allowances. This
is a modest sum of money, usually $1,000, which is set
aside immediately for the widow and her dependent,
unmarried children, to tide them over until the assets
of the estate are distributed. Obviously, such a small
sum is inadequate to support a widow and small children while the estate is being settled. The testator concerned about his family's needs after his death will
want to make certain they will be able to live during
this transitional period. One of the more obvious means
is ample life insurance. In addition, there should be
sufficient funds in a joint checking account to allow the
family to live on a modest scale for a least six months
to a year. The amount of life insurance and the sum in
the joint checking account will depend, in part, on the
age of the wife, her ability to work, whether or not she
has an independent income, the resources of her husband, and the number of children. Certainly, an indi-
spensable part of any estate plan should be a sufficient
amount of life insurance to protect both the wife and
the minor children, with the wife and/or children being
made the beneficiaries. Since insurance companies pay
death claims promptly, this is one of the best methods
of making certain that the family will be provided for
after the testator's death.

6. *Your home.* If the house in which you live is
titled in your name and in that of your spouse with
right of survivorship, the home automatically goes to
the survivor without the need of either a will or pro-

bate. But suppose the house is titled in your name alone. Do you wish the home to go to your surviving spouse completely and forever? Or do you wish her to have it only during her lifetime and then pass to the children after her death?

7. *Legacies.* There are two kinds, general and specific. The former is a sum of money given to someone. "I give and bequeath the sum of $5,000 to my brother Charles if he survives me" is a general legacy. How would you wish it paid, in a lump sum or in installments? A specific legacy, on the other hand, reads as follows: "I give and bequeath to my son, Charles Cotton, the diamond wrist watch I inherited from my father."

The distinction between a specific and a general legacy is important. In the first place, the executor is generally not entitled to a commission on the value of the diamond wrist watch. In the second place, a specific bequest has priority over a general bequest. In the third place, if at the time of the testator's death he no longer owns the wrist watch, the legacy is considered adeemed and the son would receive neither the watch nor its equivalent in cash. Ademption or adeemed means that the bequest has failed or been revoked.

But a cash bequest, which is a general legacy, is paid out of the general assets of the estate, those not specifically bequeathed, even though the testator may not leave any cash. Another important distinction occurs when the testator does not leave sufficient property to pay all the general legacies. Although the specific legatees receive all items earmarked for them (assuming they are still owned at the time of the testator's death), the general bequests are all proportionately diminished or abated. The word abatement means reduction. Assume that in your will you leave $5,000 each to your three sisters. If there are assets of only $10,000 to take care of these bequests, each of the legatees will have her share cut down proportionately and will receive one-third of $10,000 or $3,333.33, unless you direct otherwise in your will.

If you leave real estate to one person and cash bequests to others and there are insufficient assets, the bequests will be cut down proportionately but not the real estate. In other words, the person to whom you devised the real estate takes it without contributing to the legatees' bequests. You can control this situation by stating in your will that you wish certain bequests to be paid in full even though others cannot be made at all. In this situation you must name the gifts that are to have priority.

8. *Gifts.* Interesting questions arise concerning gifts to debtors and creditors. Suppose that during your lifetime you loaned your brother $5,000, for which you have his promissory note. Do you want your executor to collect the debt? If so, place the promissory note among your valuable papers where it is likely to be found. It may be that your brother is as poor as the proverbial church mouse, so poor that you have left him $10,000 in your will. Do you want your brother to have the $10,000 plus the $5,000 you originally loaned him or the $10,000 less the $5,000 loan? If you want your brother to have both the $10,000 bequest and the note cancelled, say so clearly in your will; if you do not, your executor will pay over the $10,000 less the $5,000 due on the promissory note.

Similar thought should be given to the more unlikely prospect of your making a gift to one of your creditors. Is the gift to be in lieu of the sum due him or in addition? This is something you will have to determine for yourself.

9. *Advancements.* The same principle applies to advancements as to gifts. Assume that during your life-

time you gave one of your children $25,000. In your will you leave him an equal amount. Was the original $25,000 a gift or an advancement? If it were a gift, your child would still receive the $25,000 left him in the will; if it were an advancement, he receives nothing since you paid him the money during your lifetime. In the latter case there must be some evidence such as book entries or promissory notes on which the executor of your estate can proceed.

10. *Business.* Special problems are posed if you own a business. Do you want it liquidated after your death, or carried on by your spouse or someone else? Is your spouse capable of running the enterprise or of engaging someone to run it for her? Does she need the income from the business to help her survive financially?

A client I knew owned a small but highly successful drug store. An indifferent businessman, he was helped considerably by his shrewd, aggressive wife who had a flair for merchandizing and salesmanship. In his will the pharmacist left everything to his wife. Upon his death she converted the drug store into a lucrative package liquor and cut rate patent medicine shop which not only provides her with an income but, equally important, keeps her active and busy.

If you are in business with an associate, are both of you covered by sufficient life insurance with which to purchase the deceased's interest in case the other dies? These and many more questions arise when a business is involved.

11. *Charity* You may be inspired to leave something to your favorite charity or organization. There are a few cautions. One is that you should use the correct corporate title of the recipient. "I give and bequeath the sum of one thousand dollars ($1,000) to The ABC Hospital, Inc., in the city of Baltimore, state of Mary-

land." A second is that in some states some unincorporated institutions are unable to take a gift under a will. A third is that a gift to an institution for a specific purpose (e.g., for research into the marriage customs of the aborigines of Australia) may be impractical. Your bequest could be insufficient for the purpose intended, or the college, university, or hospital could have more pressing and immediate needs. Even if your gift were accepted at the outset, it could be discontinued later because the project was no longer feasible.

When you have a specific purpose in mind, a good way to leave a charitable gift is to insert the following paragraph in your will. "I give and bequeath to the ABC Hospital, Inc., in the city of Baltimore, state of Maryland, the sum of $5,000 for research into emphysema. However, I attach no restrictions to said gift and if in the judgment of the trustees of said hospital such a project is impractical, then the same $5,000 may be used for general purposes of the aforementioned hospital."

People are charitable for a variety of reasons, obvious or not so obvious. Some give to expiate a sense of guilt, some to better their public or private image, some with mixed motives. Whatever the reason, charitable gifts are usually tax deductible. They are either exempt from inclusion in the first place or deductible from the gross estate. In any case, where a charitable gift is contemplated it should be checked against the Internal Revenue Code as well as applicable state laws to secure full advantage of any tax benefits.

12. *Trusts.* In a later chapter I discuss trusts in detail. Here, I merely wish to focus the reader's attention on some important questions. Do you wish to leave all or any portion of your estate in trust or is the entire corpus to be distributed once and for all?

If your decision is to create a trust for your spouse, giving the income but not the principal, further questions arise. When do you want the trust to begin? How much income is to be given and for how long? Is it to be disbursed weekly, monthly, quarterly, semi-annually, or annually? If the income does not meet needs, will you allow an encroachment on the principal, especially in case of some emergency such as illness? If your spouse re-marries, would you prefer that the trust be terminated and go to someone else? What becomes of the trust when the beneficiary dies? These are important questions you must first resolve for yourself; then you can seek your attorney's guidance in making decisions.

There are similar questions relative to a trust for a child. During the child's minority who is to get the income? When will payments be made? What arrangements will you make for emergencies, travel, education? If the trust permits encroachments on the capital, to what extent and for what purposes? If the trust is for a daughter, is it terminated on her marriage? Is she ever to get the principal? Is the income her separate property beyond the reach of her husband? In case she dies will the trust go to her children, if any, and in what proportion? If the trust is for a son, will you allow the trustee to invade the capital to enable your son to go into business, buy an automobile, or invest in stocks and bonds? What about a spendthrift trust (about which more later) to protect him or her from encumbering the income? How long should the trust continue? Who is to get the principal amount after the trust is ended?

You may wish to consider a trust for some other relative, for example a parent who is ill or unable to support himself or who needs a supplemental income.

Here again you are confronted with such questions as how long is the trust to last, when are payments to be made, who is to get the income upon the death of the parent? What disposition will be made of the principal?

In creating a trust you have to consider not only the beneficiary but the trustee. What powers will you give him to handle the estate, broad and discretionary or narrow and limited? Will you insist that he be limited to the securities you leave at the time of death (growth stocks, for example) or allow him to convert into utility or other income producing investments? Can the trustee sell real estate without an order of court? Must he sell publicly or be allowed to sell privately?

If you are a surviving spouse, the question arises of a guardian for your minor child. There are several possibilities. In your will you can appoint one person to be the guardian both of your child's person and of any property you leave him by testamentary disposition. You may also name co-guardians, one for your child's person, another for his property. If you choose a competent guardian, he will be confirmed by the court, ohterwise the court will name someone in his place.

Trouble frequently occurs when a surviving spouse names a stranger as guardian for his minor child. A grandparent, uncle, aunt, or other relative may object that the blood relative has closer ties than the stranger, understands the child better, and has more empathy and understanding. It is then for the court to decide, having the child's best interests in mind, who shall be guardian of his person and of his property.

You can avoid the necessity for a property guardian by having your lawyer insert an infancy clause in your will. This may be used in cases where the child is to receive only income from a trust. Under such a clause the trustee is authorized to use his discretion in paying out to the minor as much income as he thinks necessary and wise. He may disburse such income directly to the minor or to the minor's personal guardian. Any surplus is accumulated in the trustee's account for the benefit of the ward. The entire accumulation must be turned over to the ward when he or she reaches the age of twenty-one. This arrangement has the advantage of avoiding a guardian's commission and bond while at the same time preserving the infant's estate, not inconsiderable benefits, which you should discuss with your attorney.

13. *Common disasters.* What happens if a husband and wife are killed simultaneously in an automobile or airplane accident? Without a will, the property or estate will be distributed as if each person had survived. This means that the husband's estate will be apportioned according to the laws of intestacy of his state, and the wife's estate will be similarly distributed.

For example, a husband and wife owning their home as joint tenants with right of survivorship are killed in an airplane crash. Assuming there is no will the property is cut in half, the husband's share going to his kin, the wife's portion to hers. A wife is named as primary beneficiary in a life insurance policy taken out by her husband, and the policy provides that in case of the wife's death the proceeds are to be paid to the children or to the husband's estate. When both husband and wife die simultaneously in an airline crash, the proceeds will be divided equally between the children and the husband's estate.

A sound precaution to insure that property goes where intended is to have the following clause inserted in the husband's will: "If my said wife shall die simultaneously with me or under such circumstances that it is impossible or there is insufficient proof to determine who predeceased the other, I direct that my wife shall be deemed to have predeceased me and that the provisions of this will shall be construed upon that presumption, notwithstanding the provisions of any law establishing a different presumption of death."

14. *Disinheriting your spouse.* The best advice I can give you is "don't." The rule of law is that if a husband and wife are legally married and live together, each has a claim to a certain share in the other's property. You can determine that share by consulting the rules of intestacy for your particular state in chapter 3. In short, a spouse has the right to elect to take against the will and receive the share he or she would have received if the spouse had died without a will.

Assume that a husband and wife are both residents of New York, and the husband has an estate of $250,000 mostly in common stocks. In his will he leaves his wife $5,000. The elective share in New York is one-third of the net estate of the decedent if there are one or more children and one-half of the decedent's estate if there are no children. If the wifes takes under the will, she will receive only $5,000. If she takes against the will and there are no children, she will receive one-half of her husband's estate. Obviously, she is better off to take against the will.

To avoid the necessity for election, one spouse should leave the other at least the minimum allowed under the laws of intestacy, which vary from state to state.

It is possible for a husband to disinherit his wife from any share in his real property in Alabama, Arizona, District of Columbia, Florida, Georgia, Michigan, North Carolina, North Dakota, South Carolina, South Dakota, Utah, and Wisconsin. He may disinherit his wife from personal property in Alaska, Arizona, Delaware, Florida, Georgia, Michigan, New Jersey, North Carolina, North Dakota, Oregon, Rhode Island, South Carolina, South Dakota, Utah, and Wisconsin.

A wife may disinherit her husband from her real

property in North Dakota and South Dakota. She may disinherit him from personal property in Alaska, Delaware, Georgia, New Jersey, North Dakota, Oregon, Rhode Island, South Carolina, South Dakota, and Utah.

Theoretically, there are several ways to get around a spouse's right of election. One method is by way of an antenuptial or prenuptial agreement, or what is known and favored in Europe as a marriage settlement. Here is what such an agreement looks like:

"This agreement made between John Doe, herein called the First Party, residing at _____ in the city of _____ state of _____, and Mary Smith, herein called the Second Party, residing at _____ in the city of _____ state of _____ witnesseth as follows:

A marriage is about to be entered into between the parties hereto. In anticipation thereof they desire by prenuptial agreement to fix and determine their respective rights in each other's property and estate of any nature or description arising out of the marriage.

In consideration of the premises and of the mutual covenants and conditions herein contained, the parties agree to the following:

One. The First Party hereby accepts the provisions of any last will and testament which may be hereafter made by the Second Party in full discharge, settlement, and satisfaction of any and all other right, title, and interest which he, as the Second Party's husband, might acquire in her estate and property but for such testamentary provision and the provisions of this agreement.

Two. The First Party waives and releases unto the Second Party, her executors, administrators, or assigns, any and all right or rights of election given to him as the husband of the Second Party to take against her last will and testament under any statutes now or hereafter in force in this or any other state in which the Second Party may have property at the time of her death or in which the parties or either of them may reside.

Three. The Second Party hereby accepts the provisions of any last will and testament which may be hereafter made by the First Party in full discharge, settlement, and satisfaction of any and all other right, title, and interest which she, as the First Party's wife, might acquire in his estate and property but for such testamentary provision and the provisions of this agreement.

Four. The Second Party hereby waives and releases unto the First Party, his executors, administrators, or assigns, any and all right or rights of election given to her as the wife of the First Party to take against his last will and testament under any statutes now or hereafter in force in this or any other state in which the First Party may have property at the time of his death or in which the parties or either of them may reside.

Five. The parties shall take any and all steps and shall execute, acknowledge and deliver to each other any and all instruments which may be necessary to effectuate the purposes of this agreement.

Six. This agreement shall become effective when and if, and only when and if, the contemplated marriage between the parties actually takes place. If the marriage does not take place, this agreement shall be and become wholly null and void.

In witness whereof, the parties hereto have set their hands and seals this _____ day of _____ in the year of _____ in the city of _____ state of _____.

_____ (SEAL)
John Doe

_____ (SEAL)
Mary Smith

Witnessed by:

_____
As to John Doe

_____
As to Mary Smith

To be valid a waiver or antenuptial agreement must be entered into freely and with full disclosure of the facts. There must be no fraud or trickery. Walter Smartaleck, a wealthy widower in love with a gorgeous cutie half his age, tells his dearly beloved that he is worth $50,000 when he is actually worth $500,000. He persuades his girl friend to sign a waiver of her rights to his property for $10,000, which he gives her in the form of a certified check. A few months after the marriage Walter dies of a coronary. Whether or not Walter left a will, his widow can attack the waiver and have it set aside on the ground that there was no full disclosure of Walter's property, if she can prove that she was induced to sign the agreement under false pretenses.

An election is not automatic. It must be made in writing to the personal representative of the decedent's estate within the prescribed period set forth in the statute, which varies from state to state.

The right of election is not absolute. It may be lost by a wife who deserts her husband without just cause or by a husband who fails to provide for his wife's support. If the husband and wife are legally divorced, the ex-spouse has no claim against the decedent's estate, but the problem becomes more involved if the divorce is questionable or of the quickie variety.

A prominent businessman went to Mexico, where he obtained a divorce without his wife's knowledge, consent, or approval. A few days after the divorce he married a much younger woman who had been his mistress and made a new will disinheriting his children and his first wife. He left his estate of more than a million dollars to his second wife. A few weeks later the testator died. The first wife contested the divorce on the ground that it was obtained fraudulently and without notice, and the will on the ground that it deprived her of her marital rights. Fortunately for the second wife, who might otherwise have lost everything, a compromise was effected by attorneys representing both sides. The divorce was allowed to stand and the second wife was given twenty-five percent.

Suppose you are not divorced from your spouse but merely separated? Is your spouse still entitled to a portion of your estate? The answer depends on whether or not there is a valid separation agreement. If the parties had voluntarily agreed to separate and a written separation agreement was drawn up and approved by both parties with each side represented by counsel, the agreement would ordinarily have provided that each party waive whatever rights he or she had to the property of the other. Under such circumstances each party may execute a new will. A mere separation without a valid agreement containing a waiver of property and other rights leaves the parties still man and wife, and as such each is entitled to share in the other's estate.

The rules, however, are not uniform from state to state. It is always wise to consult an attorney to determine what an ex-spouse or one from whom you are separated may claim from your estate.

15. *Disinheriting your children.* Whenever one spouse leaves his entire estate to the surviving spouse, he has in effect disinherited his children. There may be persuasive reasons for doing so. The usual one is that the youngsters are too young or otherwise unable to handle property, and your wife will properly provide for their education and welfare.

Other reasons for disinheriting a child may be that you have made a settlement on that child during your lifetime, that the child is an adult with sufficient income of his own, or that there is some serious personal reason prompting the disinheritance.

Whatever the reason, the law allows you the right to cut off a youngster without leaving him anything. It is customary, and sometimes obligatory, to mention the child's name in the will and to give the reason for not leaving him anything. A simple statement to the effect that "I give, devise, and bequeath my entire estate, real and personal, to my wife Ann, knowing that she will make ample provision for my children" is sufficient. Similarly, a statement that "I leave nothing to my son David because I have not heard from him the past five years" will effectively cut him off from your will.

A new will should be executed after the arrival of each child although many states now provide by law for after-born or adopted children. The principle generally applicable is that they shall take the same share they would have taken had the testator died intestate, if they are not mentioned or provided in the will itself.

In New York if the testator has children but neither mentions nor provides for them in his will, after-born or adopted children cannot share in the estate. If, on the other hand, provision is made for one or more living children in the will, subsequent children are given an equal share with those already mentioned. If at the time of the will there is no child in existence, an after-born or adopted child takes the share he would have received had their been no will.

All this does not prevent you from barring an after-born or adopted child providing you specifically exclude him from your will.

An illegitimate child usually inherits from and through his mother. It may inherit from the father if the paternity of the father is established or if the father marries the mother.

To sum up, you should execute a new will whenever you marry, divorce, or are widowed and upon the birth or adoption of each child.

16. *Husband and wife.* I have previously alluded to the fact that it is not necessary for the testator to discuss the provision of his will with anyone. There

may, indeed, be reasons for not doing so. The testator may wish to leave a spouse the minimum provided by law, may not wish to disclose business affairs, or may be on bad terms emotionally and unwilling or unable to communicate with a spouse.

But where a marriage has been tested by time, where genuine affection and respect exist, it is desirable for the husband and wife to discuss their business affairs. There are practical reasons for this. An attorney who prepares a will may be severely criticized by the surviving spouse for not safeguarding his or her interest or may be accused of unduly influencing the testator. Given such a situation the surviving spouse may be prompted to dissent from the will and make probate difficult and expensive. Since the odds favor a wife surviving her husband, he should at least listen to her ideas about providing for the family. In many cases I have found a husband can profit from his wife's practical suggestions for the support of herself and the children.

17. *Remarriage.* A problem that often arises in will making is the question of remarriage. Consciously or unconsciously, many men dislike the notion of their wives remarrying after their death and do whatever they can in their wills to make such a venture impractical. You cannot prevent the remarriage of a surviving spouse as that is against public policy. However, it may be unprofitable for the surviving spouse to rewed if the terms of a trust agreement change. The testator can provide that if his widow remarries she will receive only a child's portion of the income, the balance going to the trustee for the support and education of the children. Such a stipulation would prevent an unscrupulous second husband from living on the children's share of the father's estate or from laying his hands on the wife's share of the principal.

A jealous or vengeful husband may dictate that in the event of the wife's remarriage she will forfeit the entire income from her husband's estate. If he does, a part of the benefits of the marital deduction will be forfeited. In addition, the wife may then elect to take either under the trust agreement in the will or her intestate share. Again, the testator may provide that on a spouse's remarriage the house shall be treated as part of the general estate. Such a provision could prevent a second husband from moving into the family home and upsetting the life of the children of the first husband.

In all cases the question of remarriage of the surviving spouse is of such a delicate and technical nature that it should be thoroughly discussed wtih a competent attorney.

CHAPTER 8

CONTESTING THE WILL

Your lawyer may write the most careful will in the world, but this will not prevent someone from trying to upset it. It may be an aggrieved son or daughter who had been disinherited, a brother or sister who has been given a smaller share, or a surviving spouse.

Contesting a will is expensive and might even be successful. In any event it will have to be defended by the executor of your estate, which bears the costs. To guard against attacks many wills contain clauses disinheriting anyone who contests the will in any of the following ways:

1. Opposes probate of the will.

2. Institutes proceedings which declare any of the provisions of the will null and void.

3. Refuses to join in the application for probate of the will.

4. Refuses to accept the gift or devise under the will.

5. Denies that it is the testator's last will and testament.

6. Questions the validity of any of the gifts or devises.

7. Denies the will was properly executed.

8. Schemes to obtain a larger portion of the estate than that to which he is entitled.

9. Fails to resist such proceeding to the full extent of his ability.

A successful attack on a will may have the following consequences:

1. Any or all legacies may be revoked in favor of the caveator, the one seeking to upset the will.

2. The caveator's share may go to some other named beneficiary.

3. A contesting child's share may be divided among the children who assent to the will.

4. The contestant's portion may fall into the residuary estate.

5. The contestant's portion may be barred from any share of the estate.

6. The contestant may be cut off with $100 or some other nominal sum.

7. The estate may be divided as if the contestant had died before the testator and the gift to him lapsed.

8. The gift to the contestant may be reduced to what he would get under the law of intestacy.

If you anticipate trouble from some relative, your lawyer should include a clause or paragraph penalizing the person contesting the will. Here are some sample paragraphs that may accomplish that purpose.

"If any objection shall be made to the probate of this will or any attempt made to revoke the probate by any of my heirs, next of kin, legatees, devisees, or any beneficiary under any provision of this will, or in case any contest shall rise as to carrying into effect any article thereof, it is my will that any heir, next of kin, legatee, devisee, or beneficiary under any provision of this will who shall make or offer or permit to be made or offered any such objection or attempt or who shall inaugurate or raise or abet any such contest shall by reason thereof forfeit any and all right or interest which he or she might have in my will or in my estate, and shall be excluded from any share or interest in my estate as legatee, devisee, heir at law, next of kin, or otherwise, and I hereby give, devise, and bequeath the property, interest, articles, or money constituting such devise, legacy, or share in my estate to which he or she might otherwise become entitled to such of my residuary legatees as shall not have violated this provision of my will."

A simpler method of accomplishing the same purpose is the insertion of the following sentence: "In case any of the devisees or legatees mentioned in this will shall contest this will, his, her, or their interest thereupon shall be forfeited and the legacy or devise shall be null and void and become part of my residuary estate."

Another way to discourage unwarranted attacks on wills is to saddle the costs on the contestant. Here is one way to accomplish this: "I direct that in case any litigation whatever arises in respect to this will or any of its provisions or its probate or concerning the trusts hereby created or any of them, all the costs, disbursements, and allowances awarded by the court to all the parties concerned in such litigation and also all the costs, disbursements, counsel fees, and expenses of every name, nature, and description, which may be incurred by the executors of or the trustees under this will in defending or preparing to defend any such legal proceedings or in taking advice with respect to their right and duties concerning the same or with respect to the construction of this will or any question growing out thereof, shall be charged against the amount coming under this will or otherwise from my estate to the persons commencing or joining such legal proceedings against the said executors or trustees and shall be considered as so much money paid to such person or persons as applied to their use with like effect in every respect as if the same amount of money or its equivalent had been paid, transferred, or conveyed directly to them by my said executors and trustees. The statement of the amount paid or incurred by my said executors as aforesaid shall be accepted as conclusive upon any accounting by them with respect thereto, both as to the reasonableness of any counsel fees and as to the correctness of all payments made." While such a provision may not hold up in all the courts, it may persuade a beneficiary to accept what he was originally given rather than risk the expense of litigation which could exceed that amount.

These are two things worth remembering. One is that no matter what you say, you cannot keep a determined individual from contesting your will. The other is that every contestant does not necessarily disinherit himself. It is true that if the contestant fails to upset the will, he may be penalized. But if he succeeds, he may receive a larger portion of the estate than that granted him under the will. If the will is successfully attacked, the entire will may fail and the estate be distributed as if no will at all had been written.

There are usually six grounds for contesting a will:

1. The will was not legally executed.

2. Testator lacked the mental or physical capacity to make a will.

3. Testator was the victim of undue influence.

4. Execution of the will was procured by fraud.

5. The will is a forgery.

6. The will, though valid when made, was later revoked.

All of which brings me to another point. Try to plan your will calmly and objectively, preferably with the assistance of an experienced attorney in whom you have confidence. Many testators are prone to invite will contests by cutting off someone for a grievance, real or imaginary. A father may be displeased with a rebellious son or with a daughter he thinks has married beneath herself socially or financially. These may be legitimate grievances or they may be passing moods which do not deserve to be perpetuated forever in one's will.

Here is where a good lawyer can perform an immense service. First of all, he should not prepare a will when the client is obviously emotionally disturbed. Nor should he allow the testator to execute a will that is palpably unfair or unjust. This does not mean the lawyer should dictate the terms of the will or decide how the estate is to be divided or administered. A good lawyer's function is to advise and counsel, to help his client think clearly and calmly about his family and dependents.

Any lawyer can prepare a will which will dispose of your property. But it takes an altogether different breed to guide you in disposing of your worldly goods with wisdom, justice, and propriety.

CHAPTER 9

ABOUT TRUSTS

You have a problem. You have a large estate, a wife, and three children. For one reason or another you do not wish to leave your estate outright to your family. But you do want them, on your death, to receive the income from the principal or corpus of your estate.

To accomplish this the law allows you to bequeath property in your will to a designated person called the trustee, who may be either an individual or a trust company. Depending on your instructions in the trust agreement, he will invest the proceeds of your property and distribute the income for a designated period to the beneficiaries you name in your will. After the specified period is over, he will distribute the principal sum to whomever you have named in your will.

Because of the fiduciary or confidential relationship of the trustee, he is held to a high degree of responsibility. He must obey the instructions of the trust agreement and he must obey the law. He may not, under any circumstances, use trust funds for his own purposes.

Basically there are two kinds of trusts, (1) the testamentary trust such as the one mentioned above that is established under the provisions of a will, and (2) the living or *inter vivos* trust, which is set up by a person during his life time to take effect immediately.

In the living trust you simply transfer property to an individual or trust company. Under a written agreement you, for example, arrange to pay income to your wife during her life and provide that after her death the principal shall go to your children in equal shares. The *inter vivos* trust becomes effective the moment the property is transferred to the trustee.

Living trusts are either revocable or irrevocable. If revocable, it allows you to see how well the arrangement works while you live, so that you may alter or revoke the agreement if it works unsatisfactorily. A revocable trust avoids the expenses of probate and of gift taxes because, since it is revocable, it is not a true gift. Under an irrevocable trust, you lose complete control. It is subject to gift taxes but not to death or federal estate taxes.

In this book we are concerned only with testamentary trusts.

Obviously, if your estate is small there is not much point in setting up a testamentary trust. A principal of $20,000 invested at six percent will yield an annual income of $1,200. The beneficiary would be better off if you leave the money outright.

Trusts are for people who leave substantial estates with income that is meaningful to the beneficiary involved. But what is adequate income for one person may be completely inadequate for another, depending on the individual, style of living, and other sources of income.

Whether you leave your estate outright or in trust is a question to decide for yourself. There are no hard and fast rules to cover all family situations. In making the judgment whether to leave income or principal or some combination thereof, take into consideration the age, skill, drive, intelligence, experience, and circumstances of the proposed beneficiary.

An elderly parent left $100,000 outright would be

better off with a set annual or monthly income to cover living expenses, supplemented by Social Security benefits.

A child who has considerable artistic or literary talent might be better off with an annual income, so that he or she could pursue his painting or writing unencumbered by financial worries or responsibilities.

In situations like this, some fathers are apt to be unreasonable, forcing their own desires on their youngsters. I know one case where a promising novelist was left a large business in which he was not at all interested, and under his management the concern rapidly deteriorated. Had the father left his son an annual income, the latter might have made a major contribution to the American novel.

One of the arguments against the creation of a trust is that it destroys ambition and initiative if the person is young. If, happily, you leave in trust one million dollars which yields an annual income of $60,000 for your son, there may not be much incentive for him but to enjoy wine, women, and song. Your son can become a professional playboy, join the international jet set, and devote his time and energy to the art of doing nothing on a lavish scale.

Another argument against a trust is that the testator's hard earned money goes to strangers for administrative expenses without exceptional results. This author knows a case where the beneficiary, a son, lost all because the trust company officer made stupid decisions and lost what had been a thriving business. What should be remembered is that a trust company is only as good as the trust officer administering the trust. There is no reason why, when setting up a trust, you should not only inquire into the background of the trust company but into the credentials of those who will manage the trust itself after you are gone.

The major purpose of a trust fund is the protection

of beneficiaries. It follows that a trust should be created for those who, for one reason or another, should not be saddled with business responsibilities. Such persons may include the surviving wife, children, elderly parents, unsuccessful brothers, and unmarried sisters. These should be the testator's first concern.

Let's consider the wife. If you have a substantial estate, your first problem is to determine what your wife will need after your death. Will there be sufficient money from your insurance, Social Security, and other sources to meet her living expenses? Keep in mind increasing costs resulting from continuing inflation.

If you can calculate what she will need to live on after your death, the rest is relatively simple. Set up a trust fund by which the trustee pays the widow a monthly or quarterly allowance. This way she will know exactly what she has and can budget her income. She may not be able to live in luxury, but hopefully you will have provided for her basic needs.

The disadvantage is that you may not be able to foresee future conditions. What about emergencies, such as serious illness and hospitalization? Or travel? Since a trust agreement can be elastic, the powers of a trustee narrow or broad, you can provide that in case of any named emergency the trustee may encroach on the principal to take care of the contingency. You can also allow your wife discretion with which to encroach on the principal. Of course, the more the principal sum is encroached the more the income is reduced and the less is left the remainderman—the one who gets the principal sum after the trust is terminated.

If you wish to allow your wife to invade the principal of the trust fund, your attorney should include a paragraph along the following lines: "I hereby authorize my trustee from time to time to pay over to or apply for the benefit of my wife so much or all of the principal of the trust as my trustee may in his absolute discretion deem advisable, which payments and applications shall be absolute and free from all trusts. The judgment of my trustee as to the amount of such payments or applications and their advisability shall be final and conclusive upon all persons interested or who may become interested in such trust. Upon making any such payments or applications my trustee shall be fully released and discharged from all further liability or accountability."

If you leave both a surviving widow and children, should there be one trust fund or two? The better practice is to divide the trust funds into two, which will protect the youngsters in case the widow later remarries. You can also provide in the trust agreement that so long as the wife remains a widow she shall receive the entire income for the support of both herself and the children but that upon remarriage she shall receive a child's share, or that upon remarriage her portion shall be equally divided among the children.

Certain questions arise when you set up a trust fund for children, especially if they are under age. Should the child receive a stated income each month, quarterly? Should the amount be disbursed from income only or from capital as well? Should the youngster receive all the income available, or only that sufficient for maintenance and education? Since the needs and expenses of a child increase from year to year, it is a good idea to allow the trustee broad authority to increase payments. A six-year old youngster will require less than a teenager. A youngster going to college will require considerably more.

In allotting the trust income to a youngster consider the following. First, you do not know exactly what your income will be after death. Second, a prudent trustee may be able to increase the income as well as the principal of the estate by wise investments or these amounts may diminish. Third, it might be unwise to give a youngster income in excess of his requirements. Finally, the trust should have sufficient elasticity to allow for invasion of capital in case of real necessity.

Among the practical questions when a trust is established for a child is to whom shall the trustee pay the income. It may not be feasible for the child to receive it directly. He may not have the necessary discretion, and the trustee may not be able to supervise every expenditure—books, records, clothing, and medication.

There are some solutions, however. If the mother is alive and the child lives with her, the trustee can make payments to the mother on behalf of the child. If the mother is not living or is incompetent, the trustee can have the court appoint a guardian for the minor's person to whom payments can be made. A third possibility, if the child is at school or college, is for the trustee to make necessary payments directly to the school or college itself.

Whatever the solution, a trustee cannot act unless he is granted broad powers on behalf of the minor child. You might have your attorney include a paragraph such as the following: "If any of my aforementioned children shall be minors during the term of this trust, then the income belonging to such child shall be paid to my said wife or to the guardian of the person of such minors during their minority to be used for the care, maintenance, and support of such child during his or her minority, and after such child shall attain majority, such child's income shall be paid to him or her during the remainder of the trust."

This paragraph represents another way of handling the problem: "I direct that the application of any income to the support, maintenance, or education of any beneficiary of any trust hereinbefore created during the minority of such beneficiary may be made by said trustee in such manner as he thinks best, either directly by the trustee or through payments to the guardian of any such beneficiary, or to the person with whom such beneficiary may reside. The receipt of such guardian or person shall be a full discharge of said trustee for all moneys which it may think best for the support, maintenance, or education of such beneficiaries through payments made to the guardian or the person with whom he or she may reside."

Another question the testator has to answer is when the principal of the estate shall be delivered and the trust ended. When the child reaches 21? When he is 25? When he has completed college? At the time of his marriage? When he is ready to go into business or begin a professional career? The fact that a child reaches 21 does not necessarily mean that he is ready to take over an estate. In fact, a child may not mature until 25 or 35, or he may never mature.

You could empower your trustee to let him distribute the estate at various times as and when he thinks best. Or you might decide that your son or daughter should receive the income only between ages 21 and 25, one-third of the principal between 25 and 30, another third between 30 and 35, and the final portion at some later specified age.

The following paragraphs are sample instructions in a will:

"When my said son shall arrive at the age of 21 years, to pay over to him all the accumulated income and one-fourth of the principal of my estate, provided my son shall have manifested by that time such habits of thrift and good judgment that my trustee shall be convinced that he will use wisely the portion of the principal of my estate paid over to him; but if my son shall not have manifested by that time such habits, then I direct my trustee not to pay over to him any part of the principal but to pay over to him the accumulated income only and to continue to pay over to him annually or quarterly or as often as my trustee shall think best the income until he shall arrive at the age of 25 years.

"When my son shall arrive at the age of 25 years, to pay over to him one-third of the then principal of my estate and in addition to pay over to him discharged of the trust out of the balance of the principal of my estate that amount which shall be equal to the amount he shall have accumulated between the ages of 21 and 25 by his own efforts—that is to say, by his honest labor and not by speculation—and as to this my trustee shall be the sole judge; provided, however, that unless my trustee shall be convinced that my son at the time he arrives at the age of 25 years shall have acquired such habits of thrift and sound judgment in business affairs that he will wisely use the estate delivered to him, then my trustee shall not pay over to him any part of the principal of my estate but shall continue to pay him annually or quarterly or as often as my trustee shall think best only the income of my estate.

"When my said son shall arrive at the age of 30 years, pay over to him all the balance of my estate—principal and accumulated income—discharged of the trust, provided my trustee shall be convinced that he has acquired such habits of thrift and shown such sound judgment in business affairs that he will wisely use the estate; but if my trustee shall not be so convinced of the thrift and good judgment of my son, then my trustee shall not pay over to him any part of the principal of my estate but shall continue during the period of his natural life to pay over to him annually or quarterly or as often as my trustee shall deem best the income of my estate.

"If my trustee in carrying out the provisions set forth in the above paragraphs shall continue to hold my estate or any part of it in trust during the period of the life of my son, then at the death of my son, leaving issue, my trustee shall continue to hold the estate in trust and pay the income to or for the benefit of said issue until the youngest of them shall be 21 years of age and then shall close the trust by paying over the principal to the issue, share and share

alike; and if my son shall die without issue, then to close
the trust by paying over said fund, principal and income,
to the board of trustees of the ABC Hospital, Inc., in the
city of Baltimore, state of Maryland, to be used by them
for the general objects of that institution.

"So that my son may not feel aggrieved but may understand and sympathize with my motive in leaving my estate
in trust for him instead of giving it outright to him at my
death, I state that I am endeavoring to avoid the risk of his
dissipating his estate by unwise management while he is
young and immature, to relieve him of the burden of managing a large estate, such as mine is and his will be, while
he is immature; and leave him free to complete his education and decide the business or profession most suitable to
his taste and aptitude, and all the while to make the estate
itself serve as an incentive to him to develop habits of
thrift and acquire, by a gradual instead of a sudden impo-
sition of responsibility upon him, a sound judgment in
business affairs. I would have my son understand and ap-
preciate that my sole aim in the execution of this will has
been his highest welfare."

The so-called spendthrift trust is another device to
restrict the beneficiary, its prime purpose being to prevent him from having full control of either the income
or the principal of the trust fund created for his benefit.

Anyone can sell or assign his anticipated benefits
under a will, and there is an active business of buying
a remainderman's expected receipt of principal at ab-
surdly low prices. A spendthrift trust may prevent this,
depending on the laws of the state in which it is drawn.
Within limits you can accomplish the following objectives:

1. Revoke a gift if the beneficiary attempts to assign
or pledge it.

2. Declare that both principal and income shall not
be subject to any claim or demand against the beneficiary or subject to any debt or contract made by him.

3. Declare that no interest of the beneficiary shall be assigned in anticipation of payment or be liable in any way for his debts.

4. Declare that if the beneficiary shall attempt to dispose of income or if because of bankruptcy or other cause the beneficiary shall be unable to enjoy the income but allows it to pass to someone else, the trust shall cease and the trustee shall apply the income for the personal support and maintenance of the beneficiary at the trustee's discretion.

5. Declare that the trustee shall not be accountable to any person other than the beneficiary directly and personally.

6. Declare that the trust shall not be subject to attachment, garnishment, or levy, and that it shall not pass to an assignee, trustee, or other person under any bankrupt or insolvent law.

7. Declare that payment shall be made to the beneficiary personally and only upon written receipt of such beneficiary free from the claims of creditors of the beneficiary.

Where the law allows and you fear that the spendthrift will be taken advantage of, your lawyer will want to include a paragraph along the following lines: "Each and every beneficiary under this trust is hereby restrained from and is and shall be without right, power, and authority to sell, transfer, pledge, mortgage, hypothecate, alienate, anticipate, or in any other manner affect or impair his, her, or their beneficiary and legal rights, titles, interests, claims, and estates in and to the income and/or principal of this trust during the term hereof. Nor shall the rights, titles, interests, and estates of any beneficiary hereunder be subject to the rights or claims of creditors of any beneficiary nor subject nor liable to any process of law or court. All of the income and/or principal under this trust shall be transferable, payable, and deliverable only, solely, exclusively, and personally to the above designated beneficiaries hereunder at the time entitled to take same under the terms of this trust. The personal receipt of the designated beneficiary hereunder shall be a condition precedent to the payment or delivery of the sum by the said trustee to such beneficiary."

As a further precautionary measure and as a deterrent to the beneficiary who attempts to do what you forbid in the spendthrift trust, you can provide that the income from the trust shall no longer be paid to the beneficiary but shall go to someone else either named by you or specified by the trustee.

A final argument in favor of trusts concerns certain tax advantages. Property bequeathed or devised outright will be subject to certain estate taxes as well as the cost of administration. When the original beneficiary dies leaving the estate again, your estate is in fact taxed a second time with a second set of administration costs. If, however, you provide in your will that your beneficiary is to have only the income during life with the principal then going to your children, your estate is taxed only once, upon your death.

Remember that the creation of a testamentary trust is a complex legal document calling for a high degree of skill and precision. It should be drawn only by an experienced attorney. To do otherwise is to invite confusion and disaster.

Chapter 10

TRUSTEES AND WHAT THEY DO

The trustee's job begins where the executor's leaves off.

The primary function of an executor is to *settle* an estate. He gathers together all the properties, determines what debts are due, and pays those the estate owes. He makes inventories, appraisals, reports, returns, and accountings, sees that all income and estate taxes are paid, manages and supervises the property during the year of settlement, and finally makes distribution according to the terms of the will.

After the estate is distributed, the function of the executor ends. A trust may continue for several generations before the fund is finally liquidated and the proceeds distributed.

In a typical trust the testator leaves a sum of money to the trustee. The trustee, in turn, is the legally responsible manager of the fund and invests it according to the terms of the trust agreement. The income from the fund is payable by the trustee to the testator's wife for her life. After her death the income goes to the testator's only child for his life. Upon the latter's death the trust ends and the principal is then paid to some other designated beneficiary, called the remainderman. In legal parlance the testator's wife is the life beneficiary, the testator's son is the second life beneficiary, and the person, persons, or charitable organization is the remainderman.

Generally the trustee's powers are limited to those set forth in the trust agreement. These may be either broad and discretionary, narrow and limited, or somewhere in between.

An example of a trust with broad and discretionary powers is one in which the testator in effect tells the trustee to run the estate as if it were his own, to make investments without hindrance, to do whatever is necessary to increase both income and principal within the limits allowed by law but without other restrictions. The trustee is held free from liability in case of faulty judgment. Obviously such broad powers should be entrusted only to someone in whom you have the highest degree of confidence.

An example of a trust with narrow and limited powers is one with detailed, written instructions on exactly how you want the trust managed. The trustee is told what he can and cannot do, what investments he can make and those he is forbidden to make, exactly what property should be invested and how, when, and to whom the income is to be paid, how much is to be spent for the education of each child and even the schools and colleges each child is to attend. In such a trust the testator has little confidence in the judgment of the trustee and directs virtually his every move.

Between these extremes is the kind of agreement in which the testator does not bind the trustee with rigid and inflexible rules but suggests ways and means by which the testator's objectives can be achieved. He will instruct the trustee, for example, that he wishes his wife and children to have a certain, fixed income but that in case of emergency the trustee may dip into the corpus or make an advancement of income to the beneficiaries. The testator will indicate a preference for certain common stocks but allow the trustee to use his discretion to switch into other type securities when market conditions warrant.

Aside from the terms of the trust responsibilities are imposed by law. The trustee must:

1. Administer the trust solely in the interest of the beneficiary.

2. Not delegate to others acts which he himself can reasonably be required to perform.

3. Maintain accurate accounts and records of the trust property.

4. On request provide the beneficiary with complete and accurate information as to the nature and amount of the trust property, including records, vouchers, and other documents.

5. At the minimum exercise such care and skill in administering the trust as a man of ordinary skill and prudence would exercise. If the trustee has greater skill and prudence than the ordinary man (such as an attorney or trust company), he is held to a higher degree of responsibility.

6. Take and retain control of trust property.

7. Take reasonable steps to realize on claims which are part of the trust estate.

8. Keep the trust property separate from his individual property.

9. Use reasonable skill to make the trust property productive.

10. Pay the net income of the trust to the beneficiary at stated intervals.

11. Treat all beneficiaries impartially.

12. If there are two or more trustees, both are required to participate in the administration of the trust.

Each co-trustee must prevent the other from committing a breach of the trust.

One of the strictest rules enforced is that a trustee must not personally profit from the trust. He cannot, for example, receive any commissions or kickbacks on any insurance taken out on trust property. Nor is the trustee allowed to buy trust property for his private account or sell his own property to the trust.

Said the U. S. Supreme Court (Magruder v Drury, 235 U. S. 106, 119): "It is a well settled rule that a trustee can make no profit from his trust. The rule in such a case springs from his duty to protect the interests of the estate and not to permit his personal interests in any wise to conflict with his duty in that respect. The intention is to provide against any possible interest exercising an influence which can interfere with the faithful discharge of the duty which is owing in a fiduciary capacity. It therefore prohibits a party from purchasing on his own account that which his duty or trust requires him to sell on account of another, and from purchasing on account of another that which he sells on his own account. In effect, he is not allowed to unite the two opposite characters of buyer and seller, because his interests, when he is the seller or buyer on his own account, are directly conflicting with those of the person on whose account he buys or sells."

To the general rule that it is improper for the trustee to buy or sell trust property for his own account there are three exceptions:

1. He may buy or sell such property for his own account when authorized to do so by the trust agreement itself.

2. He may do so provided all the beneficiaries enter voluntarily into such a transaction after a full disclosure of all the facts.

3. He may do so if the court, under special circumstances, authorizes such a transaction.

The first duty of the trustee is to take possession of the trust property. The executor of an estate must make an active search to locate the assets and, when the trustee receives the trust property or fund, he must make certain that he receives *all* the property due from the executor. If by the court's decree the executor is to turn over five hundred shares of Polaroid but delivers only four hundred, the trustee must make immediate demand for the missing shares. If they are not forthcoming, he must take whatever legal steps are necessary to recover the shares or their fair market value.

A second step is the collection and inventory of all securities and other valuable papers, including notes, policies, stocks, bonds, mortgages, deeds, and contracts, all of which should be placed in a safe deposit box in the trustee's name. Registered securities should also be transferred into the name of the trustee as should real estate, if part of the trust property.

The trustee must deposit all money belonging to the trust in a special bank account such as "John Jones, as Trustee for Mary Smith." If there are co-trustees, all accounts should be in joint names and there should be joint withdrawals.

The idea is to prevent the intermingling or confusion of a trustee's individual property with that belonging to a trust.

Third is the collection of claims. If the trust administers an apartment house, notice must be sent to all tenants notifying them of the trust and advising them that on or after a certain date all rents are to be paid directly to the trustee. If the trust runs a going business, the trustee must notify all persons who may owe money to the estate. He may employ legal counsel to collect any claims because, if they become uncollectible, the trustee may be personally liable.

Where the trust agreement provides, the trustee must manage the real estate. If the property is small, he may manage it himself. If the property is large or substantial, as in the case of an office building or apartment house, he may employ a real estate agent as manager. The trustee will also make certain that real estate under his control is fully covered by insurance, lest he be held personally liable in case of loss. If the roof leaks or there is a broken window pane, the trustee can make the necessary minor repairs without further authority.

The case may be different, however, when a once handsome building has deteriorated in a slum area to the point where it is virtually useless. Is the trustee obliged to replace the dilapidated building with a new one? Much will depend on the instructions contained in the trust agreement as well as surrounding circumstances. To protect himself against personal responsibility the trustee should obtain the court's approval in any case involving major repairs or capital expenditures.

In any trust agreement the rights of the beneficiary prevail. He is the real owner of the trust property, and the rules of law are spelled out for his protection and benefit. Hence, he has a legally enforcible right to information, to a full accounting of the assets, income, and disbursements in the trust estate. The remainderman has similar rights.

A beneficiary can demand to see the trustee's records and accounts, his books and receipts, and if not fully satisfied, can have his own accountant check the trustee's statement. If necessary, the beneficiary can go into court and compel the trustee to make a full disclosure of all the pertinent facts. He may file suit against the trustee for any alleged wrongdoing, for example, if the income is not paid on time, if it is less than the full amount, if the assets of the estate are being wasted or misappropriated.

A wrongful act of the trustee may be authorized, or later ratified, by the beneficiary. He may, for example, authorize the trustee to compromise certain claims against the estate or make investments not designated in the will. Provided the trustee has disclosed all the facts, this relieves him of personal liability. Only the consent of all the beneficiaries constitutes a valid waiver.

The death of a beneficiary under a trust agreement raises the question of who gets the income. To provide against such a contingency, it is customary to include a provision that on the death of a named beneficiary the trust agreement ceases as to that beneficiary's interest. In the usual case the income is then paid over or distributed according to the terms of the trust agreement. This could provide that the interest of the deceased beneficiary go to an alternate or substitute beneficiary, or that it go to the remainderman, which would terminate the trust.

Without such a provision, the beneficiary's interest reverts to the testator or his heirs. If the beneficiary has an interest which continues after his death, he may state in his will who shall receive that interest, otherwise, his interest goes to his heirs under the laws of intestacy.

If you have confidence in your trustee, allow him rather wide latitude about your investments, including real estate, mortgages, government and corporate bonds, and preferred and common stocks. This is especially true for corporate trustees, whose business it is to invest millions of dollars annually for their trust fund clients. Corporate trustees employ experienced investment analysts and advisers, and their collective judgment and experience in the intricacies of the stock market is apt to be far better than that of the average individual.

If you do not wish to tie the hands of your trustee, you should allow him to include the following paragraph in the trust agreement: "I hereby authorize XYZ Trust Company to invest and reinvest any funds in my estate or any trust created thereby in any property, real and personal, including without limitation stocks and other securities of any nature, without being limited to investments authorized by law for trust funds." Without such broad discretion, your investments may suffer.

No testator can possibly forecast market conditions five, ten, or twenty-five years after his death. There are bear markets and bullish ones, a time to go in for growth stocks and a time for income producing securities. In a period of inflation it may be wise to shift from common stocks into high yielding corporate or municipal bonds. Given wide discretion in the matter of investments, a trustee can take advantage of shifting financial and economic conditions and plan accordingly. He can better achieve the testator's objectives as set forth in the trust agreement.

Since a trust may last for several generations, your choice of a trustee can be crucial. This is a field for experts, not for a member of the family no matter how well intentioned. When you consider that even experts make mistakes, the wise choice of a trustee is even more imperative.

Basically your choice is probably between your attorney, in whose business judgment and skill you have the utmost confidence, and a trust company. Choosing an attorney has disadvantages. First, lawyers are mortals and hence die, at which point you are forced to choose another lawyer unless you have made provision in the trust for an alternate. Second, the average lawyer has other interests and is not exclusively concerned with the management of estates. Third, the attorney may lack the necessary skill and experience to make wise investment decisions.

Managing and conserving an investment fund is the principal business of a trust company. Its investment advisers are in close touch with market conditions. They have background and experience, and their entire time is devoted to the business of making investments, something the average individual or attorney can hardly afford to do.

If you have a substantial estate, you may wish to consider co-trustees, your lawyer and a trust company. But even here there are disadvantages. Division of authority produces divided responsibility. There may be irreconcilable conflicts between the individual and the trust company as to the best investments. Who is to decide? How are disputes to be resolved? Who is to make a decision in case the individual trustee is out of town or out of the country on a extended stay? If you insist on co-trustees, allow the trust company to have exclusive management over all investment decisions with the individual trustee having only a limited and not final say as to types and kinds of investments.

Finally, a word about fees. Compensation for trustees is fixed by the laws of each of the fifty states. If the trustee is also the executor or administrator of the estate, he is entitled to both a fee as executor and a fee as trustee.

Fees allowed trustees in New York are fairly typical. For trusts created under wills of persons dying before August 31, 1956, the commissions are:

Receiving and paying out principal, six percent of the first $2,000; three percent of the next $10,000; two and one-half percent of all sums above $12,000.

Collecting income, six percent of the first $2,000 in each year; three percent of the next $10,000; two and one-half percent of balance.

Annual principal commissions, $1.75 per $1,000 on the first $50,000; 75 cents per $1,000 on the next $350,000; 50 cents per $1,000 on all additional principal.

For trusts coming into existence after August 31, 1956:

Annual commissions, based on the value of the principal at the end of the period, $5 per $1,000 on the first $50,000; $2.50 per $1,000 on the next $450,000; $2 per $1,000 on balance of principal.

Paying out principal, one percent.

Paying out accumulated income, two percent of first $25,000 and one percent of balance at time of distribution.

In New York if the principal amounts to $100,000 or more, each trustee is entitled to a full commission unless there are more than three trustees. When required to collect rents and manage real estate, a trustee is allowed six percent of the rents in addition to the trustee's commission.

A good trustee, even more than an executor, is worth his weight in gold. You are paying him for his expertize just as you pay a skilled surgeon or an able attorney. Considering the important and complicated work a trustee has to perform and the often important decisions he has to make, the trustee earns whatever fee the law allows.

CHAPTER 11

HOW TO CHANGE OR REVOKE A WILL

You can change or revoke your will as often as you like once it is properly drawn and executed, but you must do so in the manner prescribed by law. The mere intent to change your will is not enough. Any change by way of erasure or interlineation made by you after you execute a will has no legal effect at all except perhaps to invite litigation.

If, after writing your will or having your lawyer draw one up for you, you tell your wife that you intend to die without a will, her statement would be inadmissible to prove that you intended to revoke the will.

Many testators have the curious habit of tampering with their wills after they have been properly executed. They have been known to insert words between lines, add sentences at the end of the will, erase paragraphs, run a pen or pencil across lines they disapprove of, and indulge in other antics. I have known testators to physically cut out portions leaving nothing but remnants.

There is a wrong way to change or alter a will and a correct procedure. If you are dissatisfied with your present will, do one of several things. Burn or otherwise physically destroy the document, have a completely new will drawn, or add a codicil to your existing will.

The law insists that you have the same mental capacity to revoke a will that you had when you made one. If you were reasonably sane when you executed your will but were mentally incapacitated when you attempted to revoke your will, the revocation will fail.

The act of revocation must be complete. If in a mood of petulance you begin to tear your will then repent and paste it back together, the law will generally presume that your intent to revoke was not completed, and the patched document will be admitted to probate.

If your will is in the hands of your lawyer, you do not have to ask him to return it. You can have another will drawn by another attorney. It is your last will that counts. The same is true of trust companies. If your will is on deposit with a trust company and you wish to change trustees, it is not necessary to have the trust company return your will. You can have a new one drawn anytime you like naming another trustee.

You can partially revoke a will by codicil, which is a sort of amendment to a will. It must be signed and witnessed with all the formality of an original will. The codicil should identify the old will, stating the date when it was executed, and indicate the changes to be made.

Codicils are used to bequeath a sum which has lapsed by the legatee's death leaving the money to the children, to devise land purchased after the date of the original will, to devise real estate contracted to be bought after the execution of the original will, to reduce a legacy by the amount of advances made to the legatee, to substitute for their parent the children of a son who has died, to revive a will revoked by the testator's marriage and make a devise and bequest to the wife, to revoke a will in the possession of a third party, to revive a will previously revoked, to appoint a new executor and/or trustee.

A codicil may read as follows:

"I, _____, of _____ do hereby declare this writing to be a codicil to my last will and testament, bearing date the ____ day of _____, 19____.

Whereas, by the said will, paragraph six, I gave and bequeathed to my niece, _____, the sum of _____ dollars:

And whereas, my said niece, _____, has since died and her said legacy has lapsed,

I do now hereby give and bequeath the said sum so bequeathed to my said niece, _____, as aforementioned, to and among such of her children as shall be living at the time of my death, equally to be divided between them, the share or respective shares to such child or children to be paid, assigned, and transferred to them when they shall respectively reach the age of 21 years. I direct that the interest of the said sum shall, during such suspense and payment, be applied by my executors toward the maintenance and education or otherwise for the benefit of such children respectively. And I do hereby ratify and confirm my said will in all other respects.

In witness whereof, I have hereunto set my hand and seal this _____ day of _____, 19____.

_____ (SEAL)

The foregoing instrument, consisting of two pages, was at the date thereof subscribed at the end by _____ in the presence of the undersigned attesting witnesses, and the said testator at the time of subscribing his name thereto did declare to the undersigned attesting witnesses that the foregoing instrument was a codicil to his last will, and thereafter we, the undersigned, as such witnesses signed our names hereto at the request of the testator, in his presence, and in the presence of each other.

_____	_____
Name	Address
_____	_____
Name	Address
_____	_____
Name	Address

In general codicils to wills are to be avoided or used with great caution.

There is no harm in adding a codicil if all you want to do is name a new executor to replace one who has died. If you want to revoke a legacy, on the other hand, your best bet is to draw a new will. Otherwise, you may run the risk that the original legatee will contest the probate of the codicil.

There are practical reasons for avoiding all but the simplest of codicils. One is that both the will and the codicil are placed on the public record and may cause embarrassment. A second is that the more documents to be probated, the more witnesses to be located to give testimony.

Finally, once you have drawn a will, you should go over it periodically. Laws change, even laggard ones relating to wills and estates. Some reasons which may require you to make a new will are:

1. You may be living separate and apart from your wife.

2. The status of your children may have changed.

3. You may have instituted divorce proceedings without having actually obtained a decree.

4. You may have disposed of a small or large portion of your property, or some of your property may now be outside your will and unaffected by it.

5. You may have remarried, or secured a divorce without remarrying.

6. You may have new children by your second or third spouse.

7. You may have changed your legal residence from one state to another.

8. Some of your beneficiaries under the will may have died.

9. You may want to make altogether new provisions.

10. You may want to take advantage of changes in the federal or state tax laws.

Chapter 12

HOW TO PROBATE A WILL

The first step in handling an estate after the testator's death is the probating of the will. All this means is that the executor or the attorney representing the executor proves (which is what the word probate means) that the document offered before the court is, in fact, the last will and testament of the deceased, that it was properly executed, and that the testator was mentally competent at the time he wrote the will.

A will is probated in the county and state where the testator was domiciled or had his chief residence at the time of his death. If he had his home and business in New York but died in Italy, the will is probated in New York. If he had sold his home and business and retired to the island of Majorca, intending to remain there for the rest of his life, and died in Majorca, the will would be probated according to the laws of Spain.

A will is probated by petition to a special court concerned with the administration of estates. In some states it is known as an orphan's or surrogate's court.

Whatever the name, the petition for probate is more or less the same in all fifty states. In the petition, which is accompanied by the original will and/or a sworn copy (depending on the individual requirements of the particular state), certain declarations are made:

1. That the testator died on a certain date and at a given place.

2. That he was domiciled in the county or city in which the will is offered for probate.

3. That the names and addresses are listed of all persons who are entitled to share in the estate if the decedent had died without a will, as well as those who are beneficiaries under the will.

4. That the petitioner requests that he be appointed the personal representative or executor of the testator's estate.

Actually, although it is customary for the executor or his attorney to file the probate petition, anyone interested in the estate may do so. A person who hides, destroys, or suppresses a will may be punished criminally.

If there is no objection to the contents of the will, witnesses need not appear. This is known as probate without objection. If there is an objection, the executor or the attorney acting on his behalf files what is known as a caveat to the will. This is a formal warning to the court to have a will set aside or, if the will has already been probated, to have the approval vacated.

The usual reasons for filing a caveat are:

1. That the will is a forgery, either in whole or in part.

2. That the will was improperly executed.

3. That the will was written while the testator was subject to undue influence or fraud.

4. That the will offered was revoked, either by another will or codicil or by operation of law.

To be effective, a caveat must be filed within the time prescribed by law, usually within one year after the will has been admitted to probate. Whether it is filed before or after probate, the court appoints an administrator pending litigation (*pendente lite*) to handle the estate while the court determines the validity of the will in question.

The general rule that anyone who has a direct interest in the estate may file a caveat has three notable exceptions:

1. Those having either no interest or only a remote interest in the will, such as creditors, even though they have judgments against the estate. An executor of a prior will may not file a caveat to a subsequent will.

2. Those accepting a benefit under a will.

3. Those who have contracted not to contest the will. If all the beneficiaries under a will agree, for a valid consideration, not to attempt to upset the will, the agreement will be upheld.

No matter what the will stipulates, interested parties can get together and by agreement redistribute the estate in a way agreeable to all of them. "The settlement by compromise," said one court, "of will contests and family disputes, being calculated to avert contentions, adjust doubtful rights, contribute to peace and harmony, protect the honor of the family, and avoid litigation, is not in contravention of public policy; and, when finally and fairly arrived at, is favored both in law and in equity."

Take the case of two sisters and their brother. In his last will the father disinherited his militant son and left the entire estate to his two daughters. The son objected and employed counsel to contest the will. To avoid litigation the attorneys for the daughters and the lawyer for the son entered into a compromise in which the son was allowed to share a portion of the estate rather than have a public contest and exposure of certain unpleasant facts.

When a caveat to a will is filed and there is no compromise, a hearing is held on the issues raised. The usual issues are:

1. Whether the will was procured by undue influence.

2. Whether the will was actually read by the testator.

3. Whether the will was signed by the testator.

4. Whether the testator was mentally able to execute the will and understand its contents.

5. Whether the will was properly witnessed.

6. Whether there was fraud in the procurement of the will.

7. Whether the will was revoked by the testator.

Once the issues have been framed, either side to a caveat has the right to a jury trial. A decision is made by the jury or by the judge sitting as a jury, and the will is returned to the probate court, which is bound by the verdict. The loser, of course, has the right to appeal to a higher court.

The second step after a will has been probated or approved and letters testamentary granted is the collection of assets. Usually within three months the executor or his attorney makes an inventory including all personal and real property owned by the testator at the time of his death. Corporate stocks, debts owned by the testator, bonds, notes, bank or savings and loan accounts may be appraised by the personal representative. Other property must be valued by a court appointed appraiser.

The personal representative must file a certificate that within a specified time, usually fifteen days from the filing of the inventory, he has mailed or delivered notice of such filing to all interested persons.

A separate inventory must be made of the debts due the decedent. These include mortgages and rents which became due before the testator's death as well as those which became due after the testator's death. They are usually divided into hopeful, desperate, and doubtful or some similar classification. Action must be taken by the personal representative to recover all debts which, in his opinion or in the opinion of the court, are thought collectible.

The executor or his attorney is required to reduce all assets to possession. Like a trustee he must notify all tenants to pay rents to him, have all bank or savings and loan accounts as well as safe deposit boxes transferred into his name, and file and defend suits whenever necessary. Unless expressly granted the right to do so under the will, an executor has no right to invest the assets of the estate without the written authority of the court. Should he do so and sustain a loss, the executor is held personally responsible. Again like a trustee, an executor may not profit from the estate he is administering. In other words, he cannot buy or sell on his own behalf unless the transaction is made in good faith and at a fair price.

An executor may continue the business of the decedent, if he is instructed to do so under the will or if all the interested parties give him written permission. Without such consent he has no right to continue the business and must personally stand any losses by reason of his unauthorized act.

An executor, however, has a right to use his discretion in the compromise of any debts due to the estate; he may also sell personal property ahead of real estate. Before property can be sold it must be appraised. At a private sale property cannot be sold for less than its appraised value. At a public sale property is usually sold for the highest price obtainable, after notice of the prospective sale has been published in a newspaper for a required number of weeks. All sales must be reported and ratified by the court and may be contested for cause. The court has a right to determine whether the sale was properly advertised and fairly conducted, whether the buyer was acting as agent of the executor, whether the prices were fair and reasonable, and whether the sales were to someone other than the highest bidder.

The third step in the settlement of an estate is the payment of debts.

To accomplish this the executor or attorney handling the estate publishes a notice in the local legal newspaper advising all creditors of the estate to file their claims. The notice must be published within a specified time, usually six months before distribution is made, giving the name and address of the personal representative handling the estate. If a creditor does not file his claim within the required period, the personal representative is safe in making distribution.

A creditor may file a claim after the stipulated period, but the personal representative is relieved of liability. The creditor will have to follow the assets into the hands of the next of kin by filing a suit in either a law or equity court. He may sue any one of the general legatees. If he recovers from one of them, that legatee in turn may seek reimbursement from the other legatees. If the legatee has sold the property to an innocent purchaser for value, the latter is protected.

If a creditor has a claim against the estate and is refused payment by the executor or his attorney, the creditor's recourse is to file suit against the personal representative.

The *non claim* period is the crucial factor in determining when the assets of the estate can be distributed, and it varies from state to state. Many people have the notion that within a few days or weeks after the testator's death they can claim their share of the estate. All too often it is a shock when they learn this is not so. It takes on the average a minimum of one year to settle an estate.

Here is the *approximate* time it takes to settle an estate as well as statutory provisions for small estates. What follows does not apply to trusts.

Alabama   Six months after grant of letters if debts are paid and condition of estate permits. Where personal estate is less than $1,000, no administration is necessary, title vesting in widow and minor children.

Alaska   After six months. No administration necessary if estate is less than $1,000.

Arizona   After seven months. No administration necessary if estate is $500 or less.

Arkansas   After six months. No administration necessary if estate is less than $3,000.

California   Preliminary distribution can take place after four months if bond is posted. Final distribution can take place only after final settlement of accounts of executor or administrator. No administration necessary if estate is less than $2,000.

Colorado   After six months. No administration necessary if personal estate is less than $10,000.

Connecticut   Usually within one year. No administration necessary if gross estate is $2,000 or less.

Delaware   One year. No administration necessary if estate is less than $1,500.

District of Columbia   No time limit specified; first account must be filed within twelve months but can be filed within six months. No administration necessary if estate is $500 or less.

Florida   No specified time for closing estate, but no distribution can be made until eight months after grant of letters except at personal risk of personal representative. No administration necessary if estate is less than $5,000.

Georgia   One year or less. No special procedures for small estates.

Hawaii   One year. No administration necessary if estate is less than $3,000.

Idaho No specified time, but distribution can be made after six months. Administration unnecessary if estate does not exceed $2,500.

Illinois Seven months. No probate required if estate is $5,000 or less.

Indiana One year. No probate required if estate is $2,000 or less.

Iowa Three years for final settlement. Partial distribution may be made within six to seven months. No specific provision for small estates.

Kansas One year. No specific provision for small estates.

Kentucky Six months to two years. No probate necessary if estate is $1,500 or less.

Louisiana One year, with exceptions. Special provisions for those leaving personal property in small estates.

Maine Fifteen months. No provision for non-probate of small estates.

Maryland Eight months. Estates of $2,000 or less may be distributed after thirty days' notice to creditors.

Massachusetts One year. No probate necessary if estate does not exceed $500, with certain exceptions.

Michigan Maximum period ten years. However, person entitled to estate property may petition court for distribution after all claims against estate are paid.

Minnesota One year. No specified amount established for small estates.

Mississippi After six months. No special provisions for small estates.

Missouri Semi-annual settlements must be made within six months after grant of letters, final settlement within one year unless extension is granted.

Montana After five months. More rapid administration available if estate does not exceed $10,000.

Nebraska Partial distribution may be made six

months after grant of letters. Final distribution in sixteen months but may be extended by court.

Nevada   After three months. Summary administration may take place when estate is less than $3,000.

New Hampshire   No time limit, but customarily made after end of first year. May be made after six months with approval of probate court. Simplified administration provided for estates not exceeding $2,000.

New Jersey   One year, but estate may be distributed after six months under certain conditions. Legacies are payable within eighteen months. No probate necessary if estate is $2,500 or less.

New Mexico   No specified time. No probate necessary if estate is $2,000 or less.

New York   Seven months after grant of letters, simplified procedure provided where estate is less than $3,000.

North Carolina   Two years, with exceptions. No probate necessary if estate is $1,000 or less.

North Dakota   Six months after issuance of letters. If all interested parties waive time in writing, distribution may be made sooner. More rapid distribution provided if estate is $5,000 or less.

Ohio   Six months, under certain conditions, and one month after approval of inventory. Probate unnecessary if estate is $3,000 or less.

Oklahoma   After four months, under certain conditions. Probate unnecessary if estate is under $2,500.

Oregon   No specified time. Distribution may be allowed after all claims are paid. Administration unnecessary if estate is less than $1,000.

Pennsylvania   One year, under certain conditions. Where estate is less than $2,500, it can be distributed much more quickly.

Rhode Island   Two years, with certain exceptions. Formalities dispensed with if estate is $1,000 or less.

South Carolina Fifteen months, under certain conditions. Formalities dispensed with if estate is $1,000 or less.

South Dakota Partial distribution may be made four months after issuance of letters. Final distribution may be made on final settlement of accounts or at any time thereafter on application of personal representative. Administration unnecessary if estate does not exceed $1,500.

Tennessee Twelve months, under certain conditions. Administration unnecessary when estate is $500 or less.

Texas After twelve months. Administration dispensed with if estate does not exceed $1,000.

Utah Estate may not be distributed until all claims are paid; usual period for such payment is four months. Formal administration dispensed with where estate is $1,500 or less.

Vermont Eighteen months or sooner. No special procedure for small estates.

Virginia Six months, under certain conditions. No administration necessary if estate is $1,000 or less.

Washington Five months, or after all payment of claims. No administration necessary if estate is $1,000 or less.

West Virginia One year. Formal administration unnecessary if estate is $1,000 or less.

Wisconsin Fifteen months. Simplified administration provided for, but no amount mentioned.

Wyoming No specified time, but distribution may be made after payment of claims against estate, which usually takes five or six months. County attorney administers small estates of $500 or less.

The executor has a certain number of months in which to pay the claims of creditors, but he is allowed additional time if the probate court thinks it is necessary. This may prolong the final settlement of the estate.

If the estate is solvent, creditors are all paid out of the assets of the estate. If the assets are not sufficient to pay all claims, a certain priority must be followed varying in accordance with the laws of the individual states. Typically, the priority is the following order:

1. Fees due Register of Wills.

2. Funeral expenses up to a certain amount, except by special order of court.

3. Costs and expenses of administration, including commissions of personal representatives and licensed real estate salesman and reasonable attorney's fees.

4. Family allowances, if any.

5. Taxes due by decedent, including Federal income, state income, real estate, gift taxes, Federal estate taxes, and tangible personal property taxes.

6. Reasonable medical, hospital, and nursing expenses of last illness.

7. Rent owed by decedent for not more than the statutory months in arrears.

8. Wages, salaries, or commissions for services performed within a certain number of days prior to the decedent's death.

Normally, the personal representative must make an accounting within a specified time after his appointment, typically eight or nine months, and every six months thereafter until the estate is closed. The first accounting can be the only and final accounting, depending on the law, circumstances, and the complexity of the estate. In any event, before the probate court can order legacies paid or distribution made, a final account must be stated.

The fourth and final step in the handling of an estate is the distribution of the surplus to those entitled to receive it. If there is a will, distribution is made according to the instructions contained within it. However, it should be repeated that if all the beneficiaries are of age and mentally competent and no third parties are injured, the beneficiaries may make a distribution different from that contained in the will.

Questions arise when there are sufficient assets to pay all debts, but not enough assets to pay all legacies. To find the answers it is necessary to distinguish the kinds of legacies and devises:

1. General legacies and devises.
2. Specific legacies and devises.
3. Demonstrative legacies.

If you leave your child $1,000 in your will, it is a general legacy since the amount is taken out of your general personal estate. The residuary clause, "the rest and residue of my property," is also a general legacy. If you bequeath $50,000 in unspecified stocks and bonds, this again is a general legacy. The distinguishing feature of a general legacy is that it is not a unique item but amounts from general sources. The same applies to a general devise of real estate.

A specific legacy identifies a specific item of personal property, not just money. A bequest of the eleventh edition of the Encyclopaedia Britannica is a specific legacy. So are all the books contained in your library or your automobile or stereo set. A bequest of 500 shares of A. T. and T. to your brother is also a specific legacy. If you instruct your executor to sell a property and turn the proceeds over to a designated beneficiary, the gift of the proceeds becomes a specific legacy. Again, the same applies to a specific devise of real estate.

A demonstrative legacy has some of the features of both general and specific legacies. Basically, it is a gift of a definite sum of money paid out of a specified fund. If you leave $5,000 to your son to be paid from money received from certain named securities, it is a demonstrative legacy. If you direct that such portions of your common stocks shall be sold as to produce $25,000 and the sum equally divided between your two children, each child receives a demonstrative legacy of $12,500.

An abatement is the reduction of a legacy because there are not enough assets to pay all the testator's debts or to pay other legacies having priority.

Where there is a will and not enough assets to pay all debts owing the estate, the following order of abatement usually applies:

1. Residuary personal estate will be the first to abate. This means that assets from the residuary personal estate will be siphoned off to take care of the debts.

2. Personal estate directed to be sold for the payment of debts.

3. General legacies.

4. Specific and demonstrative legacies, which contribute equally to the payment of debts.

5. Real estate charged with the payment of debts.

6. Residuary devises.

7. General devises.

8. Specific devises.

When there is a will and enough assets to pay all debts, but not enough to pay all legacies in full, the shares of each of the legatees is reduced proportionately. However, in your will you can dictate the order in which the legacies are to be paid.

If your will is silent on this point, the order of abatement is generally construed as follows:

1. Residuary legacies. The residuary clause, "All the rest, residue and remainder of my estate" takes care of surplus property otherwise not disposed of. If there is no surplus, of course nothing passes under the residuary clause.

2. General legacies.

3. Specific and demonstrative legacies, which give way at the same rate.

Ademption is the failure of a specific legacy or devise because the subject matter no longer belongs to the testator's estate at his death. It may have been lost, sold, or otherwise disposed of. If you will your house and later sell it, the gift is adeemed. If you will your son $10,000 but give him the money before your death, the bequest is adeemed.

Ademptions apply only to specific bequests and devises, not general ones. If you give ten shares of IBM, for example, and at the time of your death you no longer own ten shares, it will be bought for the person named in the will out of the general assets of the estate. If you will "*my* ten shares of IBM" but no longer own the stock at the time of your death, the gift has been adeemed and the legatee gets nothing.

What about missing heirs? Executors make a diligent search for missing heirs so they can dispose of the estate as quickly as possible. But sometimes the executor cannot locate a person legally entitled to share in the estate. To prevent undue hardships to other beneficiaries, the executor is allowed to deposit the missing heir's share with the probate court. If at the end of seven years no claimants have appeared, the money goes to the state.

Allowance is also made for distribution in advance when the beneficiary is in need. Upon petition the probate court may direct the executor or administrator to advance a portion, usually one-third, of the share to which the legatee is entitled, provided he posts bond to protect the estate against overpayment and provided the estate appears to be solvent. Similar provisions often allow a specific legacy to be turned over immediately—say, a piano—if the court is satisfied there is enough money to pay all debts.

When an estate is completely wound up, it is said to be *plene administravit*, fully administered, at which time there is nothing to do but enjoy the fruits of the vineyard. *Requiescat In Pace.*

Chapter 13

ODDS AND ENDS

Here are some questions clients ask.

An estate is subject to what taxes?

They are many. First are those the decedent would have to pay if he were living. Taking priority is the real estate tax. If it is due after death, it must be paid by the heirs. Next, is the federal income tax and after that the state income tax. These returns must be filed by the executor or administrator of the estate or by his attorney or accountant.

What are gift taxes?

Under the law a person is allowed to give away $3,000 to any one person or a total of $30,000. If he gives away more than this, he must pay a tax. A man may give his wife or a wife her husband in their life-times $60,000 of which only half will be taxable. Each parent can give a child $3,000 a year tax free, so that the two exclusions will amount to $6,000 annually. Since gift taxes are only seventy-five percent of the amount charged for estate taxes, a wealthy man is better off giving his family a considerable amount of money during his lifetime rather than let estate taxes eat it up after he has gone. Along with gift taxes which may be due the executor must also pay taxes on tangible personal property.

What taxes will the executor pay as the result of the testator's death?

The executor must pay federal and state income taxes on income received by the estate after the decedent's death.

Will you explain the federal estate tax?

It is a tax on the transfer of the entire net estate and is imposed on every estate in excess of $60,000 at the time of decedent's death. The tax is on the net, although the return must be filed whenever the gross estate exceeds $60,000 at the date of death. A forty-page return is due 15 months after the decedent's death unless time for extension is granted.

What is the marital deduction?

This provision is an important part of the federal estate tax. In a substantial estate it can result in a savings of thousands of dollars. The marital deduction provides that up to one-half of a married person's estate may be given to the spouse tax free. The deduction is allowed, however, only when the property is left so that the surviving spouse has absolute control of its disposition. For example, you leave an estate of $120,000 to your spouse. The first $60,000 is tax free under the federal estate tax law. In addition, your spouse is entitled to a tax exemption of half of your estate under the marital deduction provision, which is another $60,000, so that the entire $120,000 passes free of federal estate taxes.

Are there any state taxes which have to be paid?

Yes. Each state has its own tax laws, but the rates are generally less than the federal rates. Happily, the Internal Revenue Service allows credit to an estate for any death taxes paid to a state.

What is an inheritance tax?

This is a tax imposed by a state on the right to receive property by inheritance. Collateral heirs such as nieces and nephews often pay a higher rate than do lineal descendants such as a child or grandchild. Some states, New York for one, have abolished the inheritance tax. The tax is usually paid by the person receiving the legacy or devise, unless the will expressly provides that it shall come out of the estate.

What is the best way to provide for pets after one dies?

The simplest method is to give your pet and, if necessary, sufficient funds to take care of it during the pet's life to a reliable friend who wants the pet. You can also set up a trust for the lifetime of the trustee (not of the pet) by which you leave a certain amount of money for the support of the animal. A third method is to direct your executor to arrange for the care and maintenance of your pet after your death, leaving sufficient funds to do so.

What is meant by Widow's Quarantine?

A number of states, including New York, allow a

widow to remain in her husband's chief house forty days after his death without liability for rent and to have reasonable sustenance during that time. The allowance varies from state to state.

What is the function of a literary executor?

Basically it is to handle an author's manuscripts after his death. Ernest Hemingway, for example, has a literary executor who handles his unpublished manuscripts. Some authors leave instructions in their wills giving discretion to their literary executors on the handling of any unpublished books or manuscripts. The same discretion is often given by prominent artists and composers.

How can one make certain that funeral and burial instructions will be carried out?

The best way, of course, is to place those instructions in your will. If you want to be buried in a certain cemetery and in a certain plot and if you have made arrangements beforehand, your will is the place for expressing your preference. If you want to be cremated instead of buried, have specific ideas on how much should be spent on the funeral, on the kind of service and who would perform it, your will is the forum for your ideas.

The practical problem with leaving such instructions in your will is that the funeral may be over before the will is read by the executor. If you think this is likely to occur, you might leave your instructions in a letter to someone in whom you have implicit confidence, with instructions to open the letter immediately upon your death. Or you might make an extract of the part of your will dealing with funeral arrangements and leave it with someone you know will carry out your directions.

What should be done about one's personal effects such as clothing?

Give them to some charitable organization since members of the family may not want to wear them.

What is a mystic will?

The mystic or closed will is peculiar to Louisiana. In it the testator signs his dispositions, whether he has written them himself or has caused them to be written by someone else. The paper containing the dispositions (the will itself or the way in which he disposes of his property) must be closed and sealed in the paper serving as the envelope. The testator must present it closed and sealed to the notary and to three witnesses or he must cause it to be closed and sealed in their presence. The testator then declares to the notary in the presence of the witnesses that the paper contains his testament, written by himself or by another person at his direction. The notary then draws up the act of superscription which must be written on the paper which serves as envelope, and that act must be signed by the testator, the notary, and the witnesses.

Can aliens make a will?

Yes.

May a will be written in pencil?

Although a will should normally be typed or written in ink, a will written in pencil has been held valid. So have wills written on eggshells, bedposts, corn cribs, a navy identification disk, and a barn door!

Is it necessary to have a will notarized?

No. The notary referred to in Louisiana is much more than the notary public other states are accustomed to.

Is it a good idea to number each page of a will?

Yes, though it is not really necessary.

How about initialling each page of the will?

This also is a good idea, though again not absolutely necessary.

If a house is left to someone, does that person also get the furniture and other household effects?

Not unless you add the words "together with all of the furniture and other personal property located in my house."

Can you make a will in the form of a letter?

Yes, if such a letter is signed and witnessed by the required number of witnesses in the presence of the letter writer, otherwise not.

Index

Born February 4, 1910, SAMUEL G. KLING has practiced law in Baltimore for more than thirty-seven years and is one of the nation's foremost interpreters of law for the layman. He has contributed numerous articles to *Better Homes and Gardens, Family Weekly, Look, Parade, McCall's,* and *Cosmopolitan,* and written book reviews for the *New York Times* and the late, lamented *New York Herald Tribune.* For eight years he wrote a daily, nationally syndicated, newspaper column which was printed in more than fifty-five newspapers throughout the nation.

In addition, Mr. Kling has directed the award winning "Crime Clinic" radio program over the Mutual Broadcasting System and has been Consultant both to the Federal Prison Bureau of the U. S. Department of Justice and to the former Federal Prison Industries Reorganization Administration, under Franklin D. Roosevelt.

Besides *Your Will and What To Do About It* Mr. Kling has written a number of other books explaining law to the layman, most notably *Your Legal Advisor, Sexual Behavior and the Law, The Legal Encyclopedia and Dictionary, The Complete Guide to Everyday Law,* and *The Complete Guide to Divorce.* Mr. Kling has also contributed legal articles to the *Encyclopedia Americana.*